Dear Mom,

We thought you might enjoy this book. It is an enjoyable way to read your Bible.

Have a wonderful Mother's Day.

Lots of love,

Kathy, Jeff, Brian, Christie

DISCOVERING GOD

Other Books by Philip Yancey

Disappointment With God
Fearfully and Wonderfully Made *(with Paul W. Brand)*
In His Image *(with Paul W. Brand)*
Pain: The Gift Nobody Wants *(with Paul W. Brand)*
General Editor of The Student Bible
Where Is God When It Hurts?

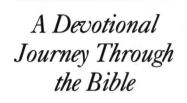

A Devotional
Journey Through
the Bible

DISCOVERING
GOD

Philip
Yancey

ZondervanPublishingHouse
Grand Rapids, Michigan

A Division of HarperCollins*Publishers*

Discovering God: A Devotional Journey Through The Bible
Copyright © 1989, 1993 by Philip Yancey

Requests for information should be addressed to:
Zondervan Publishing House
Grand Rapids, Michigan 49530

Based loosely on *A Guided Tour of the Bible: An Overview of the Bible*

Library of Congress Cataloging-in-Publication Data

Yancey, Philip.
  Discovering God: a devotional journey through the Bible / Philip Yancey.
    p. cm.
  ISBN 0-310-40240-9
  1. Bible–Meditations. I. Title.
  BS491.5.Y36 1993
  220.6–dc20   93-17947
                                                        CIP

Cover design by David Marty Design
Cover photo: ©Freeman Patterson/Masterfile
Interior design by Art Jacobs

Printed in the United States of America

93 94 95 96 97 98 99 00 01 02 /❖ DH / 10 9 8 7 6 5 4 3 2 1

 # Contents

FINAL DAYS

THE WORD SPREADS

PAUL'S LEGACY

VITAL LETTERS

Preface

This book should come with two warning stickers. First, *DO NOT ATTEMPT TO READ STRAIGHT THROUGH! Second, DO NOT ATTEMPT TO READ WITHOUT A BIBLE AT YOUR SIDE!*

Discovering God is a devotional book designed to be read at a leisurely pace, one page daily, in connection with an assigned Bible passage. Both portions can easily be read in fifteen minutes per day.

I wrote *Discovering God* after listening to many people talk about their discouragement over daily devotions and Bible reading plans. The Bible is a big book, about 1000 pages long, consisting of sixty-six different parts written by several dozen authors. Readers who approach it like any other book—beginning with page 1 and proceeding toward the end—soon find themselves lost in a bewildering maze of ancient history.

Often readers abandon the straight-through method in favor of the "hunt and peck" method. As an author, I cringe to think what would happen if people read my books in the same way they read the Bible. What if the reader picked up one of my books and arbitrarily turned to a stray sentence or paragraph on page 127? Probably it would not make sense; possibly the passage, wrenched out of its context, might convey the opposite of what I intended to communicate.

I have designed *Discovering God* to convey a sense of what the whole Bible is about. The daily readings present an overview of the Bible through 180 selected passages, including at least one chapter from each of the Bible's sixty-six books. Such a plan is no substitute for mastering the entire Bible, of course, but it may help lower barriers and point the way down a path for further study. Think of it like an introductory tour through a great art museum. You won't get to see every painting in the museum, but you will learn the basic layout, and may also acquire a taste for art that will entice you to return again and again.

With a few exceptions, I have arranged the biblical material in rough chronological order. You will read the psalms atrributed to David as you read about David's life, and the Prophets as you read about their background history. Portions from the Gospels, too, are interspersed, giving a composite picture of Jesus' life on earth; and Paul's letters are scattered thoughout the record of his life. This arrangement should help convey the Bible's "plot."

I fervently hope that this book will be one step in helping prepare you for a lifetime habit of Bible reading. A relationship with God works like any other relationship: what you get out of it depends on what you put into it. The Bible is the most important book ever written—a gift to us from God himself. If you want to discover God, and get to know him, begin here.

The Plot Unveiled

When It All Began

KEY VERSE: *In the beginning God created the heavens and the earth. . . . God saw all that he had made, and it was very good. (Gen. 1:1, 31)*

*E*verything, truly everything, begins here. The story of the Bible—more, the history of the universe—starts with the simple statement, "In the beginning God created," and the rest of the chapter fills in what he created: stars, oceans, plants, birds, fish, mammals, and finally man and woman.

Genesis 1 says little about the processes God used in creation; you'll find no explanations of DNA or the scientific principles behind creation. But the opening chapter of the Bible does insist on two facts:

Creation was God's work. "And God said. . . . And God said. . . . And God said"—the phrase beats in cadence all the way through the chapter, a chapter that mentions the word *God* thirty times. And in this first chapter, the very first glimpse we have of God is as an artist. Butterflies, waterfalls, bottlenose dolphins, praying mantises, kangaroos—they were all his idea. This entire magnificent world we live in is the product of his creative work. God, no one else, is the master of the universe, and all that follows in the Bible reinforces the message of Genesis 1: Behind all of history, there is God.

Creation was good. Another sentence tolls softly, like a bell, throughout this chapter: "And God saw that it was good." In our day, we hear alarming reports about nature: the ozone layer, polluted oceans, vanishing species, the destruction of rain forests. Much has changed, much has been spoiled since that first moment of creation. Genesis 1 describes the world as God wanted it, before any spoiling. Whatever beauty we sense in nature today is a faint echo of that pristine state.

Captain Frank Borman, one of America's Apollo astronauts, read this chapter on a telecast from outer space on Christmas Eve. As he gazed out of his window, he saw earth as a brightly colored ball hanging alone in the darkness of space. It looked at once awesomely beautiful, and terribly fragile. It looked like the view from Genesis 1.

LIFE QUESTION: *When was the last time you noticed, really noticed, the beauty of the natural world?*

Human Close-up

After presenting the cosmic view in chapter 1, Genesis 2 repeats the story of creation, narrowing the focus to human beings. We alone, of all God's works, are made "in God's image." People have disagreed over the years on what, exactly, that phrase "image of God" means. Is it immortality? Intelligence? Creativity? Relationship? Perhaps the best way to understand is to think of "the image of God" as a mirror. God created us so that when he looked upon us he would see reflected something of himself.

Genesis makes the point that human beings are profoundly different from all of God's other creations. We recognize that difference instinctively: You won't go to jail for running over a dog or cat, but you might go to jail for running over a man or woman. Human life is somehow different, more "sacred." Alone of all creation, human beings received the breath of life from God himself.

Genesis 2 shows human history just getting underway. Marriage begins here. Even in a state of perfection, Adam felt loneliness and desire, and God provided woman. From then on, marriage would take priority over all other relationships.

Work begins here, too. Adam was set in a role of authority over the animals and plants. He named them and tended to the plants and creatures of the Garden. Ever since, humans have had a kind of mastery over the rest of creation.

Only the slightest hint of foreboding clouds this blissful scene of Paradise. It appears in verse 17, in the form of a single negative command from God. Adam enjoyed perfect freedom, with this one small exception—a test of obedience.

Throughout history, artists have tried to recreate in words and images what a perfect world would look like, a world of love and beauty, a world without guilt or suffering or shame. Genesis 1–2 describes such a world. For a time, peace reigned. When God looked at all he had created, he paid humanity its highest compliment. "Very good," he pronounced. Creation was now complete.

LIFE QUESTION: *If you could design a paradise, what would it look like?*

The Crash

"The fall of man" theologians call it, but really it was more like a crash. Adam and Eve had everything a person could want in Paradise, and yet still a thought nagged them, "Are we somehow missing out? Is God keeping something from us?" Like any human being, like every human being who has ever lived, they could not resist the temptation to reach for what lay beyond them.

"There is only one doctrine that can be empirically verified," said George Bernard Shaw, "the doctrine of original sin." Genesis gives few details about that first sin. Only one thing mattered: God had labeled one tree, just one, off-limits. Many people mistakenly assume sex was involved, but in fact something far more basic was at stake. The real issue was: Who will set the rules—the humans or God? Adam and Eve decided in favor of themselves, and the world has never been the same.

Adam and Eve reacted to their sin like anybody reacts to sin. They rationalized, explained themselves, and looked for someone else to take the blame. The author of Genesis pointedly notes that they also felt the need to hide. They hid from each other, sensing for the first time a feeling of shame over their nakedness. Perhaps the greatest change of all, however, occurred in their relationship with God. Previously they had walked and talked with God in the Garden as a friend. Now, when they heard him, they hid.

Genesis 3 tells of other profound changes that affected the world when the creatures chose against their Creator. Suffering multiplied, work became harder, and a new word, *death*, entered human vocabulary. Perfection was permanently spoiled.

The underlying message of Genesis goes against some common assumptions about human history. According to these chapters, the world and humanity have not been gradually evolving toward a better state. Long ago, we wrecked against the rocks of our own pride and stubbornness. We're still bearing the consequences: all wars, all violence, all broken relationships, all grief and sadness trace back to that one monumental day in the Garden of Eden.

LIFE QUESTION: *Have you ever felt hemmed-in or stifled by one of God's commands? How did you respond?*

Crouching at the Door

Creation, the origins of man and woman, a fall into sin—in three chapters Genesis has set the stage for human history, and now that history begins to play itself out. The first childbirth—imagine the shock!—the first formal worship, the first division of labor, the first extended families and cities and signs of culture all appear in chapter 4. But one "first" overshadows all the others: the first death of a human being, a death by murder.

It took just one generation for sin to enter the world, and by the second generation people were already killing each other; the malignant results of the Fall spread that quickly. The early part of Genesis shows God intervening often in response. Here, unable to ignore the horrible changes that have crept into his world, God steps in once again with a custom-designed punishment. Cain was to bear the resulting mark with shame the rest of his life, but a few generations later a man named Lamech would brag about his murders.

Not all the news was bad. Civilization progressed rather quickly, with some people learning agriculture, some choosing to work with tools of bronze and iron, and some discovering music and the arts. In this way, human beings began to fulfill the role assigned them as masters over the created world. But despite these advances, history was sliding along another track as well. Every person who followed Adam and Eve faced the same choice of whether or not to obey God's word. And, with numbing monotony, all chose like their original parents.

God's warning to Cain applied to everyone who followed down through the generations. The next few chapters tell of an ever-worsening spiral of rebellion and evil.

LIFE QUESTION: *Note Cain's response when God confronted him. What do you think you would say if God appeared in person to confront you over some sin?*

Under Water

KEY VERSE:
Seven days from now I will send rain on the earth for forty days and forty nights, and I will wipe from the face of the earth every living creature I have made. (Gen. 7:4)

The downward cycle of sin and rebellion continued until, finally, God reached a fateful decision. Genesis 6 records it in what is surely the most poignant sentence ever written, "The Lord was grieved that he had made man on the earth, and his heart was filled with pain." It seemed clear that the human experiment had failed. God, who had taken such pride in his creation, was now ready to destroy it. He could no longer tolerate the violence that had spread across his world.

Legends of a great flood exist in the records of cultures in the Middle East, in Asia, and in South America. One Babylonian document in particular ("The Epic of Gilgamesh") has many parallels to the account in this chapter. But Genesis presents the flood not merely as an accident of geography or climate; it was an act of God. The churning waters described in this chapter stand as a symbol of how far humankind had fallen. Torrents of water swept through towns and cities, forests and deserts, destroying every living or man-made thing.

Yet Noah's ark—a huge, ungainly boat riding out the storm—stands as a symbol, too: a symbol of mercy. God had resolved to give earth a second chance, which explains why he ordered Noah to meticulously preserve representatives from every species.

Genesis underscores one message above all: The first human beings on earth made a mess of things. Beginning with the rebellion in Genesis 3, the humans had brought on the downfall of all creation. And when the time of judgment came, only eight survived: Noah and his wife and their sons and wives.

LIFE QUESTION: *Many people have the idea that human nature is basically good. Do you agree?*

A New Start

KEY VERSE:

The LORD smelled the pleasing aroma and said in his heart: "Never again will I destroy all living creatures, as I have done." (Gen. 8:21)

The gloomy tone of Genesis 7 brightens almost immediately. The next chapter tells of Noah and his family landing on an earth fresh-scrubbed and sprouting new life. All the people who had so grievously offended God had died off. For the first time in years, human beings sought to please God: In his first act on land, Noah made an offering of thanksgiving.

God showed his pleasure by responding with a solemn promise, the first of several *covenants* in the Bible. The terms of the covenant reveal how deeply Adam's fall had affected all of creation. Man had cast a shadow across all nature, a shadow of fear and dread that would continue to spread throughout the animal kingdom. God's covenant recognized certain sad adjustments to the original design of the world. It took for granted that human beings would continue to kill, not only the animals, but also each other.

Despite these adjustments God promised, regardless of what might happen, that never again would he destroy life on such a massive scale. He vowed, in effect, to find another way to deal with the rebellion and violence of man, "though every inclination of his heart is evil from childhood."

An appropriate symbol—the rainbow—marked this first recorded covenant by God. Noah, like Adam before him, had a chance for a brand-new start. Honored by God's special approval, he had the opportunity to set civilization on a whole new course. But before long, Noah went the way of his predecessors—the last glimpse Genesis gives of him, he is sprawled in his tent, drunken and naked.

What seemed like a brand-new story turns out to be a tired recapitulation of the same old story of human failure.

LIFE QUESTION: *What does God's covenant with Noah teach about the uniqueness of human life?*

The Plan

KEY VERSE: *After this, the word of the LORD came to Abram in a vision. (Gen. 15:1)*

Many times God had intervened directly in human history, but almost always for the sake of punishment—in Adam's day, and Cain's, and in the days of Noah, and at Babel. After scanning these centuries of dismal failure, Genesis changes dramatically at chapter 12. It leaves the big picture of world history and settles on one lonely individual, not a great king or a wealthy landowner, but a childless nomad named Abraham.

It's almost impossible to exaggerate the importance of Abraham in the Bible. To the Jews, he represents the father of a nation, but to all of us he represents far more. He became a singular man of faith whose relationship to God was so close that for many centuries God himself was known as "the God of Abraham."

In effect, God was narrowing the scope of his activity on earth by separating out one group of people he could have a unique relationship with. They would be set apart from other men and women as God's peculiar treasures, his kingdom of priests. This special group would by example teach the rest of the world the advantages of loving and serving God. And Abraham was the father of this new humanity.

Dozens of other passages in the Old Testament set forth the details of God's covenant, or contract, with his chosen people. (The word *testament* means covenant.)

Here is what God promised Abraham: **A new land to live in.** Trusting God, Abraham left his home and traveled hundreds of miles toward Canaan. **A large and prosperous family.** This dream obsessed Abraham and, when its fulfillment seemed long in coming, tested his faith severely. **A great nation.** It took many centuries after Abraham for this promise to come true, but finally, in the days of David and Solomon, the Hebrews at last became a nation. **A blessing to the whole world.** From the beginning, God made clear that he chose the Hebrew people not as an end, but as a means to the end goal of reaching other nations.

LIFE QUESTION: *Do people still rely on "covenants," or contracts today? What purpose do they serve?*

Sodom and Gomorrah

KEY VERSE: *. . . we are going to destroy this place. The outcry to the LORD against its people is so great that he has sent us to destroy it. (Gen. 19:13)*

Like a photo negative, this chapter shows by contrast what Abraham was up against in his efforts to found a new and godly nation. His own nephew lived in the city of Sodom, a sordid place that looked on visiting strangers—angels, as it turned out—as prime targets for gang rape. Sexual violence was just one of Sodom's problems; Ezekiel 16:49 says that Sodom was "arrogant, overfed, and unconcerned; they did not help the poor and needy."

Despite Sodom's woeful condition, God was willing to let the city survive if Abraham could locate a mere ten righteous people there. Ten such people did not exist, and God's patience finally ran out. Once more he stepped in with direct punishment, not to destroy the whole world, but to wipe out two centers of evil.

In typical style, the Bible doesn't bother with scientific explanations of the destruction. Was it a volcanic eruption? The Bible does not say, and the area, now apparently at the bottom of the Dead Sea, cannot easily be investigated. Genesis stresses not how it happened, but why.

According to this chapter, Lot did not learn a lesson from Sodom. Later, in a drunken state, he committed incest with his daughters, producing two family lines that would be traditional enemies of Abraham's family, the Jews.

Jesus later used the account of Sodom and Gomorrah as a warning to people who saw his miracles but ignored them (Matthew 11). God may not always intervene so spectacularly, but this story serves as a warning that his tolerance for evil has a limit.

LIFE QUESTION: *Are any catastrophes of our time punishments from God? How would you know?*

Final Exam

Abraham is renowned for his faith, but that faith didn't come easily. Although God had shown Abraham his overall plan for the future in spectacular fashion, the actual working out of that plan included many bumps and pitfalls.

God had promised Abraham many descendants, which led to a crisis of faith. Nothing gave Abraham more delight than thoughts of his children at play. But was that promise a cruel joke God had dangled before him? At eighty-five, Abraham gave up on his wife and slept with a female servant. At least he would have one child he could call his own. Then, at ninety-nine, when God reconfirmed the original promise, Abraham laughed in God's face. Sarah pregnant at ninety?

Whatever did God want? He wanted faith, the Bible says, which means complete trust against all odds, and Abraham finally learned that lesson. God kept his promise and a son was born to Abraham and Sarah. They never lived to see their descendants multiply like the stars in the sky. But they had one beloved son, whom they named Isaac, or "laughter," as if to remind them of the very absurdity, the *miracle*, of childbirth at their ages.

Then God presented a final test of faith, a trial so severe that it made the others seem like kindergarten games. The Bible makes clear that God never intended to let Abraham go through with his plan of child sacrifice. (Years later, when the Israelites actually committed infant sacrifice, God would call it "something I did not command or mention, nor did it enter my mind," Jeremiah 19.) All along, God had provided another sacrifice, a ram caught by its horns nearby. But Abraham did not know these things as he climbed the steep mountain with his only son.

Too many times Abraham had doubted God—this time he would obey no matter what. It had taken more than a hundred years, but Abraham finally learned to trust. Ever since, he's been known as a man of faith.

LIFE QUESTION: *What is the hardest "test of faith" you have ever been through?*

The Cheater

If Abraham is renowned for faith, his grandson Jacob is renowned for treachery. A twin, he was born with one hand grasping the heel of his brother who preceded him, and his parents memorialized that scene by giving him a name meaning "he grasps the heel," or "he deceives."

In ancient times, the oldest son had two clear advantages: He would receive the family birthright and the father's blessing. The *birthright*, like an inheritance document, granted the right to be in charge of the family and its property. Jacob got the birthright away from Esau by striking a bargain with his brother who was on the verge of starvation (chapter 25).

For most people of that day, the *blessing* represented a kind of magical power that conveyed prosperity from one generation to another; for Isaac, it represented far more. He was transferring to his son the covenant blessing passed down from his father Abraham, a blessing that would one day produce a whole nation of God's favored people. This chapter records one of Jacob's most elaborate tricks: a ruse to get from his tottery father the blessing that rightfully belonged to his elder brother.

As you read these stories, you might find your sympathies leaning toward poor Esau, who got tricked out of his blessing and sold his birthright for a hot meal. But the Bible comes down clearly on the side of Jacob. Esau is blamed for "despising his birthright" (Genesis 25:34; Hebrews 12:16).

Jacob, willing to lie, cheat, and steal to get in on God's blessing, would have flunked anyone's morality test (Genesis surely does not commend those tricks—Jacob had to pay dearly for them). Yet his life offers up an important lesson: God can deal with anyone, no matter how flawed, who passionately pursues him. The story of Jacob gives hope to imperfect people everywhere.

LIFE QUESTION: *In Old Testament times, names like Isaac ("laughter") or Jacob ("grasper") carried great significance. What kind of descriptive name would fit you?*

Something Undeserved

In Romans 9, the apostle Paul uses Jacob as an example of God's *grace*. Why would God choose a cheating rascal like Jacob to carry out his plan of building a holy nation? "I will have mercy on whom I have mercy, and I will have compassion on whom I have compassion" is God's answer. Paul loved the word *grace*—it means "an undeserved gift"—because he had spent the first part of his life fighting against God's will, and yet God loved him anyway.

These two scenes show grace at work in the life of Jacob. At critical moments in Jacob's life, just as he was about to lose heart, God met him in dramatic personal encounters.

The first time, Jacob was crossing a desert alone as a fugitive. Having cheated his brother out of the family birthright, he was running away from Esau and his murderous threats. Yet God came to him with bright promises, not the reproaches he deserved. Jacob had not sought God; rather, God sought him. At that tender moment, God confirmed that all the blessings he had promised Abraham would apply to Jacob, the disgraced runaway.

The next encounter occurred several decades later, the night before Jacob was to attempt a reconciliation with Esau. In the intervening years, he had prospered and had learned many hard lessons, but as he thought about the rendezvous he trembled in fear. After pleading with God to keep his promises, he received in response a supernatural encounter as strange as any in the Bible. Jacob, the grasper, had met a worthy opponent at last: He was wrestling with God himself. After that strange night, Jacob always walked with a limp, a permanent reminder of the struggle.

Along the way, Jacob picked up a new name, "Israel," a name that put the final seal of God's grace on him. Jacob the cheat became the namesake of God's chosen people, the "Israelites."

LIFE QUESTION: *Not many people have such dramatic encounters with God. How has God met you at a time of need?*

Blood Brothers

Nobody fights like brothers and sisters—family closeness seems to rub salt in the wounds of relationships. Genesis tells of several great brotherly rivalries: Cain and Abel, Isaac and his half-brother Ishmael, Jacob and Esau. In this last story, Joseph's story, eleven brothers lined up against one.

The pace of Genesis slows down when it gets to Joseph, with the book devoting far more attention to his life story than anyone else's. Little wonder—Joseph lived one of the great adventure stories of history. A stowaway, slave, and condemned prisoner, he rose to become the number-two ruler of the greatest empire on earth. The saga all began with the near-tragic event recorded in this chapter.

As his father's acknowledged favorite, Joseph seemed curiously insensitive to the potential of his brothers' jealousy. He may even have been flaunting status by relating two dreams of his family bowing down to him. At the least, he alienated his brothers so strongly that they decided to take revenge.

The brothers' first plan involved murder. As a last-second thought, they sold Joseph instead to traveling merchants on their way to Egypt. Neither the brothers nor Joseph's grieving father, Jacob—he swallowed their story of a wild animal attack—ever expected to see him again.

God, however, had other plans. Joseph's strange dreams, which got him into so much trouble at home, would prove to be his salvation in the faraway land of Egypt.

LIFE QUESTION: *Have you ever experienced God bringing good out of what at first seemed like a disaster?*

Behind the Scenes

Genesis provides a fascinating look at a variety of ways in which God gave guidance to his people. Sometimes, as with Abraham, he would appear spectacularly and in person, or send angelic messengers. For other people, like Jacob, the guidance came in more mysterious forms: a late-night wrestling match, a dream of a ladder reaching into heaven. For Joseph, God's guidance was indirect, and probably quite mystifying.

God communicated to Joseph not through angels, but mainly through dreams, weird dreams he would hear about from such dubious sources as jail mates and a despotic Egyptian pharaoh. Yet because God revealed to Joseph the proper meaning of those dreams Joseph eventually rose to prominence. Egyptians of that day were fascinated by dreams (Archaeologists have unearthed lengthy textbooks on dream interpretations.), and Joseph the dream-interpreter soon found himself at the top of Pharaoh's government.

In Joseph's time, God mostly worked behind the scenes. In fact, on the surface it often seemed that Joseph got the exact opposite of what he deserved. He explained a dream to his brothers, and they threw him in a cistern. He resisted a sexual advance and landed in an Egyptian prison. He interpreted another dream to save a cell mate's life, and the cell mate forgot about him.

Yet, and perhaps this is why Genesis devotes so much space to him, Joseph never stopped trusting God. Joseph came to see God's hand in the tragedies of his life. Being sold into slavery, for example, eventually turned out for good. It led him into a powerful new career, and the opportunity to save his own family from starvation. "So then," he told his brothers, "it was not you who sent me here, but God" (45:8). Choking back tears, Joseph tried to explain his faith to the same brothers who had tried to kill him, "You intended to harm me, but God intended it for good. . ." (50:20).

LIFE QUESTION: *If God has an important message for you, how does he get it across or get your attention so you will understand it?*

A Long Forgiveness

KEY VERSE: *I am your brother Joseph, the one you sold into Egypt! And now, do not be distressed and do not be angry with yourselves for selling me here, because it was to save lives that God sent me ahead of you. (Gen. 45:4–5)*

The old, lingering rivalry between Joseph and his brothers came to a climax as the brothers knelt unwittingly before Joseph—so Egyptian by now as to be unrecognizable—and begged for the right to buy food. Thus began a long, anguished struggle of the heart.

Joseph could have disclosed his identity and made up with his brothers or he could have gotten revenge by ordering their executions. He did neither. He began a series of elaborate tests, demanding things from them, playing tricks on them, accusing them for nearly *two years.* All these games brought his brothers confusion and fear, and also flashbacks of guilt over their treatment of him years ago.

The drama took an emotional toll on Joseph. Five times he broke into tears, once with cries loud enough to be overheard in the next room. Joseph was feeling the awful strain of forgiveness. Finally, the brothers discovered the stunning truth: The teenager they had sold as a slave, and nearly killed, was now the second-ranking imperial official of Egypt. He held their fate in his hands.

But Joseph had no interest in revenge. At long last he was ready to forgive and welcome them all to Egypt. The brothers' reconciliation opened the way for the children of Israel to become one family of twelve tribes, a single nation. The old man Jacob, back home in Palestine, didn't know what to believe when he heard the news about his "dead" son. But, spurred on by one last personal revelation from God, he, too, headed off for Egypt.

A large family, a nation, a land—God had promised all these to Abraham and to Isaac and to Jacob. As Genesis closes, only the first of the promises has come true: Jacob's twelve sons have produced a flock of children. The Bible makes plain that these twelve were no more holy than any other sons—eleven of them, after all, had betrayed Joseph. But from this starting point, God would build his nation.

LIFE QUESTION: *What makes it so hard for us to forgive others?*

Birthing
A Nation

Time for Action

Over the next four hundred years, Jacob's family grew into a great, swarming tribe. God's plan was slowly progressing, but with one major hitch: The Hebrews now toiled as slaves under a hostile pharaoh.

God's promises to Abraham, Isaac, and Jacob had been passed down to each new generation, but who believed in the covenant anymore? Daily, they felt the whips of Egyptian taskmasters. As for the vaunted Promised Land, it lay to the east somewhere, carved up under the dominion of a dozen different kings.

At last God had had enough. "I have indeed seen the misery of my people in Egypt," he said. "Now you will see what I will do." The chapters that follow record the most impressive display of God's power unleashed on earth since creation.

First God needed a leader, and for that job he selected Moses, a choice rich with irony. As a child, the Hebrews' national hero had floated in the cattails of the Nile a hairbreadth from certain death. God had next arranged for Moses to receive the best classical education available, in the pharaoh's palace, while being nurtured—for pay!—by his own Israelite mother.

It took forty years in Egypt and forty years in the desert to prepare Moses for the leadership role. God's announcement, or "call," was an encounter Moses would never forget: a fiery bush, a voice from nowhere, God introducing himself by name. "I am the God of Abraham, Isaac, and Jacob," he said, drawing a connection to all the promises that had gone before. And now the time for action had arrived. Moses was his handpicked choice to lead that mob from slavery in Egypt to freedom in the Promised Land.

As this chapter shows, Moses was far from an eager recruit. But his own resistance to God's plan was minor compared to that put up by the Israelites . . . and the Egyptians.

LIFE QUESTION: *Like Moses, do you ever wonder if certain shortcomings you perceive about yourself disqualify you for God's service?*

The Ten Plagues

To liberate the Israelite slaves, God staged a cosmic showdown known as the Ten Plagues, a showdown so dramatic that in modern times it strains the limits of Hollywood special effects crews just to depict it on-screen. A nation was aborning, and the task of uprooting the Israelites from Egypt called for outside intervention.

First, the Israelites themselves had to be convinced of God's power. Somehow God had to demonstrate that he had not forgotten his chosen people, even though he had seemed silent and unconcerned. Then, too, Egypt needed convincing: No empire would let thousands of valuable slaves walk away free. Exodus asserts more than a dozen times that the plagues were given so that the Israelites and Egyptians would recognize the power of Israel's God.

An even more basic issue was at stake: God's personal credibility. Was he just one more tribal god, like the ones the Egyptians worshiped? The plagues were, in effect, God's open warfare against the false gods of Egypt. He declared as much: "I will bring judgment on all the gods of Egypt" (12:12). Some scholars see each plague as a targeted attack against a specific Egyptian idol. Thus, the plague on the Nile River countered the Egyptians' river god; the plague of flies, the sacred fly; the plague of darkness, the sun god Ra; and the plague on livestock, the sacred bull.

The plagues began as irritants—a river turned red, frogs, gnats—and only escalated in response to Pharaoh's hardening heart. As a last resort, God inflicted the plague recorded in chapter 11. That night is remembered to this day by Jews, and also by Christians, who see Jesus as the ultimate Passover Lamb.

In the end, the plagues worked so effectively that thousands of slaves left unhindered, with the wealth of Egypt showered upon them as farewell gifts. "I am the God who brought you out of Egypt," God would remind them again and again whenever they were tempted to doubt his power or concern for them.

LIFE QUESTION: *If God declared war on the "gods" of our modern society, what would they be?*

Second Thoughts

KEY VERSE: *That day the LORD saved Israel from the hands of the Egyptians, and Israel saw the Egyptians lying dead on the shore. (Ex. 14:30)*

It didn't take long for Pharaoh and the Egyptians to second-guess their decision to release the slaves. Soon a glittering army of chariots and horsemen was charging after the defenseless Israelites.

Nor did it take long for the Israelites to second-guess their decision to leave. At the first sight of Pharaoh's army, they quaked in fear and accused Moses of leading them to certain destruction in the desert.

As this chapter tells it, the Israelites' final confrontation with Egypt was divinely stage-managed to make a point for all time: God himself, no one else, was responsible for the Israelites' liberation. More than anything else, the account of the Exodus underscores that one indisputable fact. No Israelite armies stood against the mighty Egyptians. At the last possible minute, God arranged a spectacular rescue operation, and an equally spectacular defeat of the Egyptian army. The freed captives could only respond with humility and praise; there was no room for pride. For them, independence from Egypt meant dependence on God.

That pattern of depending on God would continue all through the Exodus. When the wilderness wanderers ran out of water, God provided. When food supplies failed, God provided. When raiders attacked, God provided. In fact, the book of Exodus shows a greater proportion of miracles—direct supernatural acts of God—than any part of the Bible except the Gospels. The psalmists would never tire of celebrating these events in music, and the prophets would later hark back to the days of the Exodus to stir the conscience of their nation. The great miracle of the Red Sea merely set the tone for a national history that was from beginning to end an active movement of God.

LIFE QUESTION: *Read the song commemorating this event in chapter 15:1–18. How does it offer a good model for thanking God?*

A Treaty with God

Nearly everyone has heard of the Ten Commandments. For most of us, they represent a central core of morality, "the basics" that God requires. But for the Israelites in the desert, the Ten Commandments represented far more—nothing less than a major breakthrough. Nations around them, who worshiped many different gods, lived in constant fear of the gods' unpredictability. Who could tell what might anger or please them? But now God himself, Maker of the universe, was giving the Israelites a binding treaty signed in his own hand. They would always know exactly what God required and where they stood before him.

God held before them some wonderful guarantees: prosperity, abundant crops, victorious armies, immunity from health problems. In effect, he agreed to remove most of the problems people face in daily existence. In exchange he asked that the Israelites obey the rules outlined in this and the next few chapters. God's original covenant with Abraham he now made formal, and applied to a whole nation. (This middle part of Exodus is known as the Book of the Covenant, for it contains the essence of the Israelites' treaty with God.)

"Although the whole earth is mine, you will be for me a kingdom of priests and a holy nation," God said (19:5–6). He wanted a nation like no other, a model society centered around a commitment to him. All the Israelites waited in anticipation as Moses climbed a dark, smoky mountain to meet with God. No one present could miss the significance of that meeting: It was marked by thunder and lightning, and a loud, piercing trumpet blast, and fire. The ground itself shook as in an earthquake.

Out of that meeting on Mount Sinai came the rules summarized here. The Bible fills in more details of the treaty, but these Ten Commandments express the kind of behavior God wanted from his people. It was a day of wild hope. "We will do everything the Lord has said," the people all promised with a shout (19:8).

LIFE QUESTION: *Can you restate the negative form of some of the Ten Commandments positively? What personal rights do they protect?*

Something New, Something Old

KEY VERSE:

So Moses went back to the LORD and said, "Oh, what a great sin these people have committed! They have made themselves gods of gold. But now, please forgive their sin." (Ex. 32:31–32)

The bright hope of Exodus 20 dies forever in Exodus 32; there is no more jarring contrast in all the Bible. For forty days Moses visited with God on Mount Sinai, receiving the terms of the covenant, or treaty, that would open up an unprecedented closeness between God and human beings. But what happened down below, at the foot of the mountain, almost defies belief.

The Israelites—people who had seen the ten plagues of Egypt, who had crossed the Red Sea on dry ground, who had drunk water from a rock, who were digesting the miracle of manna in their stomachs at that moment—these same people felt boredom, or impatience, or rebellion, or jealousy, or some such mortal urge, and apparently forgot all about their God. By the time Moses descended from Sinai, the Israelites, God's people, were dancing like pagans around a golden statue.

Moses was so mad that he hurled to the ground the tablets of stone signed by God himself. God was so mad that he nearly destroyed the whole cantankerous nation.

This chapter has many parallels with the story of the very first human rebellion in Genesis 3. Both times, people favored by God failed to trust him and struck out instead against his clear command. Both times, the rebels devised elaborate rationalizations to explain their behavior. Both times, they forfeited special privileges and suffered harsh punishment.

It appeared, for a moment, that something new in the history of humanity would take place among the Israelites: an entire nation devoted to following God. Instead, the same old story replayed itself. No matter what terms God came up with, people found ways to break them.

Only one ray of hope shines out of this dark scene. Moses, the stuttering, reluctant leader, seems to grow into his position at last. His eloquent prayers are answered, and God grants the Israelites yet another chance.

LIFE QUESTION: *What do you think was really behind the Israelites' rebellion?*

Legal Matters

Leviticus seems very strange to the modern world, so strange that readers intending to read the entire Bible often bog down in this book. Unlike most of the Bible, it has few stories or personalities, and no poetry. It's a book of laws, crammed full of detailed rules and procedures.

Many of these individual rules, appropriate to God's goal of calling out a "separate" people, were changed in the New Testament. Yet a study of such laws can prove rewarding, for they express God's priorities on such subjects as care for the land, concern for the poor, and abuses of family and neighbors.

Although the Old Testament laws recorded in Leviticus, Exodus, Numbers, and Deuteronomy may seem long-winded, keep them in perspective. These laws—just over 600 in all—comprised the entire set of regulations for a nation, as far as we know. (Most modern cities have more traffic laws!) And they are brief and clear. You don't have to go to law school to understand them.

The variety of the laws shows that God involved himself in every aspect of the Israelites' life. Laws against witchcraft are mixed in with laws concerning improper haircuts, tattoos, and prostitution. God was advancing his plan for the Israelites by carving out a separate *culture.* After four centuries in Egypt, the just-freed slaves, more Egyptian than anything else, needed a comprehensive make-over. That is exactly what God gave them. (Many of the laws seem designed primarily to keep the Israelites "different" from their pagan neighbors.)

The Israelites were a unique people, unlike any other nation on earth, called by God to demonstrate holiness and purity to people around them. The reward for obeying the laws would make the Israelites the envy of the world. And if they disobeyed? God spells out in frightening detail the punishments they would then expect.

LIFE QUESTION: *Everybody has a code to live by. Where did you get yours?*

An Arm Too Short?

KEY VERSE:

The LORD answered Moses, "Is the LORD's arm too short? You will now see whether or not what I say will come true for you."
(Num. 11:23)

The book of Numbers covers a journey through the desert that should have lasted about fourteen days, but instead lasted forty years. When they first crossed into the Sinai Peninsula, the Israelites were bursting with a spirit of hope and adventure. Free at last from the chains of slavery, they headed toward the Promised Land. But the weeks, months, and then years of wandering in a hostile desert soon wore down all positive feelings.

With relentless honesty, Numbers tells what happened to change a short excursion into a forty-year detour. Petty things seemed to bother the Israelites most, as their constant complaints about food indicate. With a few exceptions, they ate the same thing every day: *manna* (meaning, literally, "What is it?"), which appeared like dew on the ground each morning. A monotonous diet may seem a trivial exchange for freedom from slavery, but read their grumbling for yourself in this chapter.

The rebellion portrayed here was typical of the whole journey. And the more childishly the people acted, the more their leaders were forced to respond like stern parents. As this chapter shows, Moses and God took turns getting exasperated by the Israelites' constant whining.

True, conditions were rigorous: Facing a constant threat from enemy armies, the tribes had to march under a broiling sun through a desert region oppressed by snakes, scorpions, and constant drought. But the underlying issue was a simple test of faith: Would they trust God to see them through such hard circumstances? Would they follow the terms of the covenant he had signed with them and depend on his promised protection?

LIFE QUESTION: *Do you ever "grumble" against God? If so, what tends to make you do so?*

Mutiny

KEY VERSE: *The LORD said to Moses, "How long will these people treat me with contempt? How long will they refuse to believe in me, in spite of all the miraculous signs I have performed among them?" (Num. 14:11)*

$\mathcal{M}$ost ancient histories record the heroic exploits of mighty warriors and unblemished leaders. The Bible, however, gives a strikingly different picture, as seen in the brutal realism of Numbers. On a dozen different occasions the Israelites lashed out in despair or rose up in rebellion, plotting against their leaders and denouncing God. The spirit of revolt spread to the priests, to the military, to Moses' family, and ultimately to Moses himself.

This chapter recounts the pivotal event of Numbers, the most decisive event since the Exodus from Egypt. The Israelites were poised on the very border of the Promised Land. If they simply trusted God, they could leave the torturous desert and walk into a land abundant with food and water.

Yet despite the miracles God had already performed on their behalf, the Israelites chose to distrust him once again. Cowed by a military scouting report of potential opposition, they loudly bemoaned the original decision to leave Egypt. In open mutiny, they even conspired to stone Moses and his brother Aaron.

The real object of revolt, the Israelites' God, felt spurned like a cast-off lover. Convinced at last that this band of renegades was unprepared for conquest of the Promised Land, he postponed all plans. The covenant promise of a new nation in a new land would have to wait, at least until all adults of the grumbling generation had died off. And that's why, out of the many thousands who had left Egypt, only two adults, Joshua and Caleb, survived to enter the Promised Land.

The Israelites had lost faith not only in themselves, but in their God. The apostle Paul points out that these failures "happened to them as examples and were written down as warnings for us, on whom the fulfillment of the ages has come. So, if you think you are standing firm, be careful that you don't fall!" (1 Corinthians 10:11–12).

LIFE QUESTION: *What "giants" cause you fear? How do you respond?*

Never Forget

KEY
VERSE:
*Only be careful, and watch your-
selves closely so that you do not
forget the things your eyes have
seen or let them slip from your
heart as long as you live. Teach
them to your children and to their
children after them. (Deut. 4:9)*

Four decades later the Israelites stood at the edge of the
Promised Land, spiritually and
physically seasoned by their
wilderness wanderings. With
the older generation of doubters and grumblers now dead
and buried; a new generation
chafed to march in and claim
the land—Egypt was a faint
memory from childhood.

There at the border, the old man Moses delivered three
speeches that, for their length and emotional power, have no equal
in the Bible. It was his last chance to advise and inspire the people
he had led for forty tumultuous years. Passionately, deliberately,
tearfully, he reviewed their history step by step, occasionally flar-
ing up at a painful memory but more often pouring out the anguished love of a doting parent. An undercurrent of sadness runs
through the speeches, for Moses had learned he would not join in
the triumph of entering Canaan.

Moses' longest speech reiterates all the laws that the Israelites had agreed to keep as their part of the covenant. Moses also
recalls the hallmark day when God delivered the covenant on
Mount Sinai. He remembers aloud the black clouds and deep darkness and blazing fire. *You saw no shape or form of God on that day,*
he reminds them. God's Presence cannot be reduced to any mere
image. Moses' central message: *Never forget the lessons you
learned in the desert.*

Besides all the warnings, Moses was giving a kind of pep
talk, a final challenge for the Israelites to recognize their unique
calling as a nation. If they followed God's laws, all the lavish benefits of the covenant would be theirs. More, every other nation
would look to them and want to know their God. Moses seemed
incurably astonished at all God had done for him and the other Israelites, and this speech represented his last chance to communicate that sense of wonder and thanksgiving.

LIFE QUESTION: *If you reviewed your own history with God, what lessons
would you learn? For what are you most grateful?*

Perils of Success

KEY VERSE:

When you have eaten and are satisfied, praise the LORD your God for the good land he has given you. Be careful that you do not forget the LORD your God, failing to observe his commands, his laws and his decrees. (Deut. 8:10–11)

Alexander Solzhenitsyn says that he had first learned to pray in a Siberian concentration camp. He turned to prayer because he had no other hope. Before his arrest, when things were going well, he had seldom given God a thought.

Similarly, Moses felt the Israelites had learned the habit of depending on God in the Sinai wilderness, where they had no choice; they needed his intervention each day just to eat and drink. But now, on the banks of the Jordan River, they were about to face a more difficult test of faith. After they entered the land of plenty, would they soon forget the God who had given it to them?

Desert-bred, the Israelites knew little about the seductions of other cultures: the alluring sensuality, the exotic religions, the glittering wealth. Now they were preparing to march into a region known for these enticements, and Moses seemed to fear the coming prosperity far more than the rigors of the desert. In the beautiful land, the Promised Land, the Israelites might put God behind them and credit themselves for their success.

"Remember!" Moses kept urging. Remember the days of slavery in Egypt, and God's acts of liberation. Remember the trials of the vast and desolate desert, and God's faithfulness there. Remember your special calling as God's peculiar treasures.

Moses had good reason for concern, for God, who could see the future, had told him plainly what would happen: "When I have brought them into the land flowing with milk and honey, the land I promised on oath to their forefathers, and when they eat their fill and thrive, they will turn to other gods and worship them, rejecting me and breaking my covenant" (31:20). As the books following Deuteronomy relate, all of Moses' fears came true.

Ironically, as Deuteronomy shows, success may make it harder to depend on God. The Israelites proved less faithful to God after they moved into the Promised Land. There is a grave danger in finally getting what you want.

LIFE QUESTION: *Do you think most about God when things are going well or when you are in trouble?*

Loud and Clear

𝓕or once, nearly everyone in the Israelite camp was jubilant. They stood, eager as children, at the edge of the long-awaited land. Moses, however, held back, unable to share the spirit of optimism. For forty years he had led this cranky tribe, and he knew them too well to think that a change in scenery would alter their old ways. A doleful sense of fatalism hangs over these last chapters of Deuteronomy. The Israelites had failed far too often; they were doomed to fail again.

Aware of the significance of this, his last chance to impress upon the Israelites the seriousness of their covenant with God, Moses pulled out all the stops. He began with the speech recorded here. The benefits of keeping the covenant Moses defined in simple and elegant terms, but as he related the consequences of breaking it, his language changed in pitch. His descriptions of those consequences are unmatched for their horror.

As if acknowledging that words were not strong enough to communicate to the Israelites, Moses also orchestrated a dramatic sequence of object lessons that would live in their memories forever. First he had the words of the law painted on some large plaster-coated stones, so that the tribes would pass by visual reminders of the covenant as they entered Canaan. Then, pre-selected shouters climbed two mountains with a narrow valley in between to yell out the rules governing the covenant. As the tribes entered the new land, their ears rang with the loud dissonance of wonderful blessings from one side clashing with horrific curses from the other.

Finally, just in case the Israelites didn't get the message, Moses taught them a song given him by God (chapter 32) and everyone memorized it.Thus at the birth of their nation, euphoric over the crossing of the Jordan River, the Israelites premiered a kind of national anthem, the strangest national anthem that has ever been sung. It had virtually no words of hope, only doom.

LIFE QUESTION: *Do the principles set forth in this chapter—"Do good, get blessed; do evil, get punished"—still apply today?*

This Time
with Courage

Often, as we have seen in the books of Exodus, Numbers, and Deuteronomy, the Israelites offer examples of what *not* to do. But the Old Testament does contain a few bright spots of hope, with the book of Joshua representing one of the brightest.

Joshua's opening scene replays an earlier scene. After listening to Moses' swan song speeches, the refugees amassed again beside the Jordan River for a test of courage and faith. Were they ready to cross into the Promised Land? Forty years before, their forebears had panicked in fear. Now, without their legendary leader, Moses, would the Israelites panic again? They had no chariots or even horses, only primitive arms, an untested new leader, and the promise of God's protection.

But an entirely new spirit characterized this group, and the spy story in Joshua 2 expresses the difference clearly. Forty years ago, sparking a revolt among the Israelites, only two of the twelve spies had held out any optimism. But the older generation with its fearful slave mentality had died off, and the new generation was now led by one of the original optimistic spies, Joshua.

This time, Joshua handpicked his own scouts, and the report they brought back makes a sharp contrast with the spy report in Numbers (13:31–33). The new scouts concluded that God had given the land of Canaan into the Israelites hands; that all the people were fearful of the Israelites. Thus Joshua begins as a good-news book, a welcome relief from the discouragement of Numbers and the fatalism of Deuteronomy. What a difference forty years had made!

The heroine of this chapter, Rahab the pagan prostitute, became a favorite figure in Jewish stories and was esteemed by Bible writers as well (see Hebrews 11:31 and James 2:25). She proves that God honors true faith from anyone, regardless of race or religious background. In fact, Rahab, survivor of Jericho, became a direct ancestress of Jesus.

LIFE QUESTION: *When you confront obstacles, are you more likely to see them as problems or as opportunities?*

Strange Tactics

The Israelites' abysmal failures in the Sinai Desert can be traced back to a simple matter of disobedience. Despite unmistakable divine guidance, they insisted on choosing their own way over God's. Would the new generation respond any differently? Once they had crossed into Canaan, God tested the Israelites' new resolve to follow him, and it must have strained their faith to new limits.

As for the residents of Canaan, who had long heard about the Israelites' plan to conquer the Promised Land, they braced for the worst. Citizens of Jericho, the first city in the invaders' path, barricaded themselves behind stone walls and awaited the feared onslaught. But how did the vaunted Israelites spend their first week in Canaan? They built a stone monument to God, performed circumcision rituals, and held a Passover celebration—not the sort of behavior you'd expect from a conquering army.

The incidents recorded in Joshua seem specially selected to strike home the point that God, no one else, was in charge. Just before the battle of Jericho, a supernatural visitor appeared to Joshua to remind him of the true commander of this military campaign. And the bizarre tactics of the Israelites in besieging Jericho left no doubt who was really in charge. An army could hardly take credit for victory when all it did was march around in circles and shout.

Jericho was probably a center for the worship of the moon god in Canaan, and so the destruction of that city—like the Ten Plagues on Egypt—symbolically announced an open warfare between the God of the Israelites and the region's pagan gods. Although measures against the Canaanites may seem harsh, the Bible makes clear that they had forfeited their right to the land. As Moses told the Israelites, "It is not because of your righteousness or your integrity that you are going in to take possession of their land; but on account of the wickedness of these nations, the LORD your God will drive them out before you" (Deuteronomy 9:5). And, as the story of Rahab shows, Canaanites who turned to God were spared.

LIFE QUESTION: *Do you ever feel foolish or strange when following what you are convinced is God's plan for you?*

Slow Learners

KEY VERSE: *Israel has sinned; they have violated my covenant, which I commanded them to keep. . . . That is why the Israelites cannot stand against their enemies. (Josh. 7:11–12)*

*T*he Bible does not record history for its own sake. Rather, it selects and highlights certain events that yield practical and spiritual lessons. For example, the book of Joshua, which spans a period of approximately seven years, devotes only a few sentences to some extensive military campaigns. But other key events, such as the fall of Jericho, get detailed coverage. That battle established an important pattern: The Israelites would succeed only if they relied on God, not military might.

Perhaps inevitably, the Israelites got cocky after Jericho. Since they had conquered a fortified city without firing an arrow, the next target, the puny town of Ai, should pose no threat at all. A few thousand soldiers strolled toward Ai. A short time later those same soldiers—minus their dead and wounded—were scrambling for home, thoroughly routed.

Clearly, the juxtaposition of these two stories, Jericho and Ai, is meant to convey a lesson. If the Israelites obeyed God and placed their trust in him, no challenge was too great to overcome. On the other hand, if they insisted on their own way, no obstacle was too small to trip them up.

Significantly, Ai stood near the original site where God had appeared to Abraham and revealed the covenant centuries before. A humiliating defeat in that place shook Joshua to the core. He dissolved in fright, earning God's stern rebuke, "Stand up! What are you doing down on your face?"

Without God's protection, Joshua realized, the Israelites were hopelessly vulnerable. After the painful lesson of Ai, he went back to the basics. The public exposure of Achan's sin underscored the need to follow God's orders scrupulously, even in the earthy matter of warfare. God would not tolerate any of the lying or looting typical of invading armies.

LIFE QUESTION: *Why would such a seemingly "little" sin, Achan's deceit, have such major consequences?*

Home at Last

KEY VERSE: *"Now then," said Joshua, "throw away the foreign gods that are among you and yield your hearts to the LORD, the God of Israel." And the people said to Joshua, "We will serve the LORD our God and obey him." (Josh. 24:23–24)*

𝒜t the end of his life, Joshua, like Moses before him, stood before the Israelites to deliver a farewell address. Things had gone well under his leadership. The Bible gives the remarkable assessment: "Israel served the Lord throughout the lifetime of Joshua." And now Joshua used his final speech to review all that God had done and to remind his people of their obligations under the covenant with God.

"I gave you a land on which you did not toil and cities you did not build"—at every point, Joshua emphasized that *God* was the sole source of their success. He had called out Abraham and blessed him with children, had delivered the Israelites from slavery in Egypt, had carried them across the desert. And in Joshua's own lifetime he had fulfilled one more promise of the covenant: He had given them the Promised Land. It was theirs to live in.

"Choose for yourselves this day whom you will serve," Joshua challenged his listeners in the stirring climax to his speech. All the people present swore their allegiance to God, the God who had kept his covenant with them. Joshua solemnly ratified the covenant and sent the people away, then quietly prepared to die.

The book of Joshua ends with an act of deep symbolism: The Israelites finally buried the remains of Joseph. For well over four centuries those remains had been preserved in Egypt in anticipation of the Israelites' return to their homeland. And during the forty years of wilderness wanderings, the tribes had carried Joseph's bones as a treasured reminder of their past. Now, at last, Abraham's descendants had come home, and even the dead could rest in peace.

LIFE QUESTION: *When you experience success, whom do you tend to credit, yourself or God?*

Leadership Crisis

KEY VERSE:
"But Lord," Gideon asked, "how can I save Israel? . . . I am the least in my family." The LORD answered, "I will be with you." (Judg. 6:15–16)

The good-news tone of Joshua sours abruptly in the next book, Judges. After an initial spurt of enthusiasm, the Israelites strayed far, very far from the way God had pointed them. Ignoring Joshua's orders to clear the land, they settled in among the pagan occupants instead. These new neighbors practiced an exotic religion that included sex orgies and child sacrifice as a regular part of worship.

Just one generation later, the Israelites had lost their sense of national identity and had forgotten all about their parents' ringing vows to honor the covenant. They, too, were worshiping the idol Baal. Having violated virtually every moral standard, the nation slid toward chaos—much like modern-day Lebanon, or Yugoslavia. The last verse of Judges sums up the scene: "Everyone did as he saw fit."

The Israelites were suffering from a leadership crisis of huge dimensions. For eighty years they had followed Moses and Joshua, two outstanding leaders who proved impossible to replace. When the twelve tribes splintered apart and retreated into separate territories, God turned to more regional leaders called *judges.* The term may be misleading; these were people renowned not for court cases, but for their military campaigns against foreign invaders. (Today they might be called guerrillas or freedom fighters.)

Some judges, such as the hero of this chapter, emerged as models of courage and faith. And yet a close look at the life of Gideon shows the material God had to work with. His family and village worshiped Baal, not the Lord. In the face of God's clear direction, Gideon sputtered, demanded repeated proofs, used delaying tactics, and worshiped at night to avoid detection. He was subject to paralyzing fears, even on the eve of battle. But God, knowing Gideon's potential, step by step brought him to the point of courage.

LIFE QUESTION: *Gideon is often used as an example of God's guidance. Do you think he's a negative or positive example? Or both?*

Raw Material

KEY VERSE:

The LORD said to Gideon, "You have too many men. . . . In order that Israel may not boast against me that her own strength has saved her, announce now to the people, 'Anyone who trembles with fear may turn back.'" (Judg. 7:2–3)

Joshua won the battle of Jericho by following orders that defied all orthodox military tactics. Similarly, when the time came for Gideon to strike a decisive blow for the Israelites, God gave instructions that would have daunted a seasoned general, much less a greenhorn like Gideon. He reduced the size of Gideon's army from 32,000 to 300 men, so as to leave no doubt it was he, God of the Hebrews, who would fight this battle.

In those days the Israelites lived at the mercy of marauding tribes of Bedouins, who would help themselves to the produce and wealth of the local farmers. But by following God's commands, Gideon led a great victory and freed his people from oppression.

Gideon's against-all-odds victory shows a pattern that is repeated throughout the book of Judges. At a time when women were regarded as second-class citizens, God chose Deborah to lead. Jephthah, another judge, had led a gang of outlaws before God chose him. In fact, this pattern appears throughout the Bible. God did not seek the most capable people, nor the most naturally "good." He worked with the most unlikely material so that everyone could see the glory was his and his alone.

The apostle Paul marveled over this principle more than a thousand years later, writing, "Brothers, think of what you were when you were called. Not many of you were wise by human standards; not many were influential; not many were of noble birth. But God chose the foolish things of the world to shame the wise; God chose the weak things of the world to shame the strong. . . . Therefore, as it is written: 'Let him who boasts boast in the Lord'" (1 Corinthians 1:26-31).

LIFE QUESTION: *Why does God so often rely on "cast offs" to accomplish his work? Who are the exceptions?*

Superman's Weakness

The most famous of all the judges makes an appearance toward the end of the book, and the Bible devotes four chapters to the dramatic events of his life. If Gideon shows how a person with limited potential can be greatly used by God, Samson illustrates just the opposite: a person with enormous potential who squanders it.

When Samson entered the picture, the Israelites were once again suffering under foreign domination. An angel announced his birth, making clear that God had great things in store for Samson and wanted him specially set apart.

Indeed, Samson was blessed with extraordinary supernatural gifts. When the Spirit of the Lord came upon him, he could tackle a lion or single-handedly rout an entire army. And yet, as the stories from his youth reveal, Samson wielded that strength in ways more befitting a juvenile delinquent than a spiritual leader.

Like any rebellious teenager, he chose for a wife the kind of woman sure to cause his parents—and God—the most grief. That marriage barely survived a week, and next Samson took up with a Philistine prostitute. This chapter describes how he, stupidly, forfeited his great strength in a dalliance with a third woman, the seductive Delilah. Samson's story is like a morality play. No one in the world could match his physical strength; just about anyone could match his moral strength. His moral lapses would seem almost incomprehensible were they not repeated by spiritual leaders in almost every generation.

In the end, Samson, the designated savior of his people, was led out to perform like a trained bear for his captors. It appeared that the God of the Israelites had been soundly defeated by the pagans and their gods. But Samson, and God, had one last surprise for the Philistine oppressors.

LIFE QUESTION: *In what areas are you living up to your potential? In what areas are you falling short?*

Tough Love

This charming tale about two scrappy women has nothing of the broad sweep of history found in Judges. Rather, Ruth narrows its focus to the story of one family trying to cope during chaotic, tumultuous times.

Things had gotten so bad in Canaan, especially after a severe famine, that Naomi's Israelite family migrated into enemy territory just to survive. There, her two sons married local pagan women and settled down. Years later, after both those sons and her husband had died, Naomi decided to return to the land of her birth. This book mainly tells of the stubborn loyalty of Naomi's daughter-in-law named Ruth.

Ruth and Naomi were unlikely friends. Ruth was young and strong; Naomi, past middle age and broken-hearted. In addition, they came from completely different ethnic and religious backgrounds. Who would have put them together? But somewhere along the way Ruth had converted to the worship of the true God, and she insisted on returning with Naomi to the land of the Israelites.

In a few brief chapters, Ruth manages to capture a slice of agrarian life in ancient times. The male-dominated society posed problems for unattached women, and these two lived in harsh, trying times. Ruth served awhile as a migrant farm worker, surviving on the gleanings left in the fields by the harvesters.

You can read this small book in several ways: as a tiny, elegant portrait of life in ancient times, or as a record of God's faithfulness to the needy, or as an inspiring story of undying friendship. (Ultimately Ruth does get a loving husband and both women find economic security.) Perhaps the most accurate way to read this story, however, is as a missionary story. God not only accepted Ruth, a member of the despised Moabites, into his family, but also used her to produce Israel's greatest king. Ruth's great-grandson turned out to be David. To anyone who thinks God's love was for the Israelites only, Ruth's life makes a striking contradiction.

LIFE QUESTION: *When has a friend "gone out on a limb" for you?*

All-purpose Leader

By the time of the judges, most terms in the Israelites' covenant with God had already been fulfilled. Abraham's descendants, twelve tribes and many thousands strong, had a land of their own. And yet, something was clearly lacking. No one could begin to call the crazy quilt of tribal territories a unified "nation." In fact, throughout the judges' era the Israelites fought each other as often as they fought their hostile neighbors.

As this book opens, the Philistines, a traditional enemy, were exploiting the Israelites' disunity, pushing ever deeper into their territory. The Philistines had superior weapons—chariots, in particular—and Israel had neither a central administration nor a regular army to mount an effective defense. A crisis of leadership was building, one that threatened the very existence of Israel. The military weakness led to one of the darkest days of Jewish history, when the Philistines captured the sacred ark of the covenant. Some wondered if God had abandoned them and forsaken the covenant.

"In those days the word of the LORD was rare; there were not many visions" begins this chapter. But it goes on to relate how God stepped in directly, as he had done with Abraham and Moses before, calling out a leader for his people. "See, I am about to do something in Israel that will make the ears of everyone who hears of it tingle," God announced. He answered the desperate prayer of Samuel, who would grow into his role as one of Israel's greatest leaders.

Ultimately, Samuel would serve in many capacities. He was both judge and prophet. A priest by training, he also led the nation's worship. When the need arose, he even functioned as a military general, spearheading a victorious recapture of disputed territories. And finally, under God's direction, Samuel anointed Israel's first two kings. By performing these varied roles, Samuel left an important legacy: He managed to unite the tribes for the first time in a century. Under his leadership, Israel came to the very brink of nationhood. God had not forgotten the covenant after all.

LIFE QUESTION: *Have you ever felt "called" by God for a certain task?*

Tale of Two Kings

The LORD does not look at the things man looks at. Man looks at the outward appearance, but the LORD looks at the heart.
(1 Sam. 16:7)

The Philistine military threat never entirely went away. As Samuel aged, Israel needed continuing vigorous leadership, but Samuel's sons hardly measured up to the task. What could be done? Looking around them, the tribes saw that virtually every other country had a king. *Aha, that's the answer,* they concluded, and urged Samuel to appoint an Israelite king (8:4–5).

The idea of a king seems to have been popular with everyone except Samuel and God, who sensed in the request an underlying rejection of God's own leadership. Samuel warned the elders bluntly against the problems they might be inviting: tyranny, oppression, a military draft, high taxes, maybe even slavery. But the people begged for a king despite his warnings.

Did God oppose the very notion of a king? Probably not. Many years before, Moses had predicted the Israelites would someday have a king, and God eventually used the royal line to produce his own son Jesus, King of Kings. But the Bible makes one thing clear: God opposed the people's motives, as expressed by the elders, "Then we will be like all the other nations" (8:20). God did not want them to be like all the other nations. He, no human being, was the true ruler of the Israelites.

Israel's first king began his reign with enormous promise. Saul was a perfect physical specimen—handsome, strong, intelligent, a head taller than anyone else. Leadership qualities oozed out of him. But he failed, for one simple reason: He disobeyed God, refusing to acknowledge him as true ruler. Without hesitating, God ended Saul's dynasty and looked elsewhere for a replacement.

The replacement king was utterly unlike the first king. No one had imagined royalty potential in the shepherd boy David— not even his own father. But, as God said, "Man looks at the outward appearance, but the LORD looks at the heart." David had the kind of heart God could work with. Despite his humble beginnings, despite his many flaws, he went on to become the greatest king in the history of the Israelites.

LIFE QUESTION: *Would the leadership qualities God values be an asset or a handicap to someone running for the U.S. presidency?*

A Shepherd's Song

KEY VERSE: *Even though I walk through the valley of the shadow of death, I will fear no evil, for you are with me. (Ps. 23:4)*

David was a well-rounded human being. Although he had enough courage to take on the likes of Goliath, he certainly did not fit any macho warrior mold. In fact, David first gained King Saul's notice for his musical, not military, skills. Initially, he was summoned to the army camp because his harp playing soothed the frayed nerves of the troubled king.

Almost half of the 150 psalms in the Bible are credited to David, and it seems only appropriate to read a sampling in conjunction with his life history. This famous psalm reveals at once the secret of David's poetic abilities and the secret of his faith.

In his poetry David tended to start with the scene around him—rocks, caves, stars, battlefields, sheep—and work out from that physical world to express profound thoughts about God. Psalm 23, for instance, stems from his experience as a shepherd boy. David was able to reduce those images to a few condensed, beautiful stanzas.

The psalm captures the essence of David's trust in God. Sheep have blind, absolute trust in a leader: If a lead sheep plunges off a cliff, an entire flock will follow. That kind of unshakable trust was what David sought in his walk with God.

Yet, no one can dismiss David as having a rosy, romantic view of life. The preceding Psalm 22 shows just how tough, gritty, and ruthlessly honest he could be. Somehow David managed to make God the center of his life, regardless of circumstances—whether he felt specially comforted by God, or cruelly abandoned. "Some trust in chariots and some in horses, but we trust in the name of the LORD our God," wrote this soldier who spent much of his time running from chariots and horses (Psalm 20:7).

The best way to read the psalms is to make these ancient prayers your own by speaking them directly to God. Over the years, millions of people have found comfort and inspiration by "praying" the eloquent words of Psalm 23, written by the shepherd who would be king.

LIFE QUESTION: *Does your faith resemble more the childlike faith of Psalm 23 or the barely-hanging-on faith of Psalm 22?*

Giant-Killer

KEY VERSE:

The LORD who delivered me from the paw of the lion and the paw of the bear will deliver me from the hand of this Philistine.
(1 Sam. 17:37)

*K*ing David dominates much of the Old Testament, and much of Jewish history. This exciting story from his boyhood, told in colorful, eyewitness detail, is one of the most famous of all Bible stories, a beacon of hope for all outsized underdogs.

David spent the better part of a decade trying to escape the wrath of King Saul, and much of Saul's enmity probably traced back to this one scene. Saul, leader of a large army, sat in his tent, terrorized by the taunts of the colossal Goliath. Meanwhile David, a mere boy too small for a suit of armor, strode out bravely to meet Goliath's challenge. Little wonder that Saul came to resent and even fear the remarkable youth.

The scenario related here is not as farfetched as it may seem. "Single combat" or "representative" warfare was an acceptable style of settling differences in ancient times. As Tom Wolfe explains it in *The Right Stuff*, "Originally it had a magical meaning. . . . They believed that the gods determined the outcome of single combat; therefore, it was useless for the losing side to engage in a full-scale battle."

During many lonely hours as a shepherd boy, David had honed his slingshot skills to a state of perfection. But he took no personal credit for the victory. "You come against me with sword and spear and javelin," he shouted to Goliath, "but I come against you in the name of the Lord Almighty, the God of the armies of Israel, whom you have defied." In the tradition of Joshua and Gideon, he placed complete trust in God alone—a lesson that King Saul had never learned.

Once Goliath had fallen, the rest of the Philistines quickly succumbed. Soon the Israelites were dancing in the streets and singing, "Saul has slain his thousands, and David his tens of thousands." The nation was beginning to recognize in David the qualities that had marked him for potential kingship. Saul, however, was not about to relinquish his throne without a fight.

LIFE QUESTION: *Have you ever been forced to rely utterly on God at a time of great fear and danger?*

Outdoor Lessons

KEY VERSE: *The heavens declare the glory of God; the skies proclaim the work of his hands. (Ps. 19:1)*

*D*avid lived much of his life outdoors. It's not surprising, then, that a great love, even reverence, for the natural world shines through in many of his psalms.

These psalms present a world that fits together as a whole. At night wild animals hunt; at daybreak humans go out to work. As rain falls, nourishing crops for people and grass for cattle, it also waters the forest where wild animals live. Yet the psalmist doesn't just marvel over the complexity and beauty of nature; behind everything he sees the hand of God. The world works because an intimate, personal God watches over it. Every breath of life depends on his will. So do the weather, the winds and clouds, the very stability of the earth.

Psalm 19 combines two of David's favorite themes: God's care for the earth, and his care for the chosen people of Israel. He begins with the natural world, marveling at the mantle of stars that covers the whole earth. Yet David and the Israelites, unlike their neighbors, did not worship the sun and stars as gods, but saw them as the workmanship of a great God who oversees all creation.

In the middle of the psalm, the author turns his attention from nature to the "law of the Lord." To reflect that change, the poem in Hebrew uses a different, more personal name for God. The first six verses refer to God with a general name that anyone, of any religion, might use, much like our English word *God.* But from verse seven onward, God is called *Yahweh,* the personal name revealed to Moses from the burning bush. The heavens declare the glory of God, but God's law reveals even more—his personal voice to his chosen people.

David wrote some of the psalms as a fugitive, while fleeing the wrath of King Saul. Even though God had promised him the throne of Israel, David had to run for his life. He had many nights of fear and many doubts, but he believed that the God who had demonstrated his faithfulness to the natural world, and to the nation David would one day govern, would show that same faithfulness in fulfilling promises to David himself.

LIFE QUESTION: *Does nature reveal "the glory of God" to you?*

Struggle for the Throne

*Y*ou can sense the force of David's personality by observing the effect he had on people around him. This chapter tells of an undying friendship from his early days, before the radical break with King Saul. The king's son Jonathan valued friendship with David so much that he forfeited his chance at succession to the throne.

Saul revealed his true, murderous intent to Jonathan in a dramatic scene at the dinner table. Jonathan warned David, and thus began the terrible struggle between the competing kings. Saul, the king rejected by God, lived on in luxury while David, secretly anointed as his replacement, lived in the wilderness, scrambling to survive. Saul had a professional army; David, a small band made up of family members and an assortment of outlaws.

The events of the next few years played out the inner character of the men. Saul knew God's will about the rightful king of Israel, but spent his life resisting it. In contrast, David showed amazing patience waiting for the prophecy to come true. Twice when Saul accidentally fell into his hands, David refused to kill him.

In the remainder of 1 Samuel, a long, Shakespearean-style drama unfolds. King Saul, an ancient Macbeth, has lost his grip and is clearly deteriorating. His son has sided with David; his daughter, married to him, has shifted her loyalties as well. Saul, insane with rage, turns up the heat. Can David hold on long enough to outlast him?

At times, David despaired. "One of these days I will be destroyed by the hand of Saul," he said (27:1). His position was desperate. David had one precious asset only: God's promise that he would be king. Although his faith in that promise was tested to the extreme, David learned to wait for God's timing. In the end, like the hero of a Shakespearean tragedy, Saul took his own life. Meanwhile, David inherited the throne of Israel.

LIFE QUESTION: *Have you ever had a close same-sex friendship such as David and Jonathan had?*

Ups and Downs

KEY VERSE: *Wait for the LORD; be strong and take heart and wait for the LORD. (Ps. 27:14)*

The psalms open a window into the inner life of King David. That window discloses some surprises, however. David was surely no saint and seldom did he show the peace and serenity normally associated with "spiritual" people. In fact, he often cried out against God, blaming him when things went wrong and begging for relief.

The psalms are not pious devotionals. They are filled with accounts of enemies who scheme and gossip and plot violence. For the psalmists, faith in God involved a constant struggle against powerful forces that often seemed more real than God. The writers frequently asked, "Where are you, God? Why don't you help me?" They often felt abandoned, misused, betrayed.

An example is Psalm 27, a psalm which shifts in mood with every stanza. The first stanza opens with a bold declaration of confidence in God from an author who seems downright fearless. The second stanza hints at the author's true condition: Tired of running, he yearns for the day when he can rest safely in God's dwelling, and rise above all his enemies. By the third stanza, all confidence has melted and the psalmist is pleading for help. The psalm ends in a calmer tone, with a word of practical advice David often had opportunity to put into practice, "Wait for the Lord."

Yet out of such trials, a strong, toughened faith in God emerged. In the years when David was an outlaw from King Saul, his hideouts included a "rock" in the desert and a "stronghold." As an experienced fighter, David knew the value of such defenses. But when he wrote about those days—as in this psalm—he called God his rock and his fortress. He recognized readily that God was the true source of his protection.

Danger did not fade away even after David became king. He faced unceasing hostility from enemies, as well as numerous internal rebellions and coup attempts. But David had learned a pattern of helpless dependence in the wilderness, and practiced it throughout his life.

LIFE QUESTION: *Is your emotional life fairly even, or full of peaks and valleys? What about your spiritual life?*

King of Passion

An unavoidable question dangles over the Bible's account of David's life. How could anyone so obviously flawed—he did, as we shall see, commit adultery and murder—be called "a man after God's own heart"? The central event in this chapter may point to an answer.

David consistently acknowledged that God, not a human king, was the true ruler of Israel, so he sent for the sacred ark of the Lord that had been captured by the Philistines half a century before. He would install it in Jerusalem, the new capital city he was building, as a symbol of God's reign.

It took a few false starts to get the ark to Jerusalem. Without looking up the regulations given to Moses, the Israelites tried transporting the ark on an ox cart, as the Philistines paraded their gods, rather than on the shoulders of the Levites, as God had commanded. Somebody died, David got mad, and the ark sat in a private home for three months.

Nevertheless, when the ark finally did move to Jerusalem, to the accompaniment of a brass band and the shouts of a huge crowd, King David completely lost control. Bursting with joy, he cartwheeled in the streets, like an Olympic gymnast who has just won the gold medal and is out strutting his stuff.

Needless to say, the scene of a dignified king doing backflips in a scanty robe broke every rule ever devised by a politician's image builders. David's wife, for one, was scandalized. But David set her straight: It was God, no one else, that he was dancing before. And, king or no, he didn't care what anyone else thought as long as that one-person audience could sense his jubilation.

In short, David was a man of *passion*, and he felt more passionately about the God of Israel than about anything else in the world. The message got through to the entire nation.

LIFE QUESTION: *If you had been in the crowd watching David dance, how would you have responded?*

A Different Kind of House

"I declare to you that the LORD will build a house for you: When your days are over and you go to be with your fathers, I will raise up your offspring to succeed you, one of your own sons, and I will establish his kingdom." (1 Chron. 17:10–11)

After bringing the ark of God to Jerusalem, David began to dream of building a splendid home for it, a temple devoted to the God of the Israelites. In a day when pagan temples ranked among the wonders of the world, he thought it only fitting to lavish the wealth of his kingdom on a "house" for the true God. But God made it clear that David was not the one to build such a temple. Elsewhere (1 Chronicles 22:8), the Bible states the reason: As a warrior, David had shed much blood, and God wanted his house built by a man of peace. That task should be left for David's son.

Although God vetoed the plan to build a temple, he granted David far more. Harking back to his covenant with the Israelites, he promised—in a tender play on words—to build a "house" out of David's descendants that would last forever. Whatever his reservations about the Israelites' demand for a king, God had fully "adopted" the king as his representative within the nation. In a typically humble response, David erupted in a prayer of astonished thanksgiving.

This promise, given in an intimate exchange between God and David, sowed the seed for what would become a long-time hope of the Jews: a royal "Messiah," or Anointed One. Saul's dynasty ended just as it had begun; David's would continue through a long line of kings and culminate in God's own Son, to be born into David's lineage in Bethlehem, the City of David. Has God's promise been fulfilled? The fact that even in modern times people still pore over the lives of David and other kings of tiny Israel—though far grander, more impressive kings have faded from history—and recognize one descendant as the true Messiah should give a hint.

(Note: The books of Samuel, Kings, and Chronicles often overlap, telling the same history from different perspectives. This chapter from 1 Chronicles repeats almost word for word the seventh chapter of 2 Samuel.)

LIFE QUESTION: *When have you felt like giving God a large gift?*

The Goodness of God

*D*avid never got over a sense of *astonishment* at all God had done for him. As he grew older and reviewed his life, he realized that, despite the hardships, God had always delivered him "from the pit." God had kept his promises. In gratitude, David wrote many psalms praising God for his past faithfulness. The king served, in effect, as a national reservoir of memory for his people; he helped the whole nation remember God's benefits.

When the Israelites praised God, their thoughts centered on God's actions in freeing them from slavery and leading them into a land of their own. Their psalms were like history lessons, designed to summon up the past, especially the hallmark days of deliverance under Moses. They studied those days in the Torah, or five books of Moses, and wrote songs to commemorate them.

The memories weren't all positive, and the Israelites' songs could be brutally frank about the ancestors' rebellions, complaints, and lack of gratitude. Yet, they had one great, happy reason to rejoice: God had kept his promise to love them. To psalm writers like David, the events of Israel's history were unmistakable signs of God's grace. They had done nothing to deserve God's love, and yet he had showered love on them.

This psalm could be titled "The Goodness of God." It reviews the dark times of illness and oppression, of sin and rebellion, and then it points with amazement to the remarkable ways in which God transformed all those dark times. God understands and will not overwhelm human weakness: "He knows how we are formed, he remembers that we are dust." More, despite our failings, he has in store for us an unfathomable eternity of love.

David has one loud message to celebrate: We do not get what we deserve. We get far more. The psalm ends in a burst of praise, starting with the grand sweep of the universe and spiraling back to the setting of the very first verse—David praising God out of his inmost being.

LIFE QUESTION: *When you review your past, do you tend to focus on the victories or the failures?*

Kings Will Be Kings

It is the simplest story in the world, this tale of David and Bathsheba: Man sees woman, man sleeps with woman, woman gets pregnant. Every year scandal sheets broadcast modern variations on the same theme. Substitute a politician —or evangelist—for the king, and a beauty queen for Bathsheba. What else is new?

The scandal didn't especially shock David's Israelite subjects. Like most people, they were resigned to the fact that the people on top who make the rules often don't bother to live by them. Lots of leaders in history have followed this course. The Romans had a phrase for such behavior, *rex lex*—the king is law—rather than *lex rex*—the law is king.

Bathsheba's pregnancy complicated the picture somewhat. Today, a leader in David's situation might destroy the evidence with an abortion. David had his own cover-up plan. It started as a clever attempt to deceive, making Bathsheba's husband appear as the likely father. Uriah's scruples, however, put King David to shame, or should have. What ensued was a classic case of "one crime leads to another." In the end, David, the man after God's own heart, broke the 6th, 7th, 9th, and 10th commandments. For his loyalty, David's soldier Uriah got the reward of murder, and many other Israelites fell with him.

This story shows David at his most Machiavellian: cold as iron, ruthless in use of his power. Even so, not a word of protest was filed. What the king wants the king gets, no questions asked.

After a mourning period, Bathsheba moved into the palace and David married her. By then many people must have surmised what had happened—the servants knew, at any rate—but the Bible doesn't report that any of them were displeased. The story of David's infidelity might have ended there, and probably would have, except for one portentous sentence at the close of this chapter. It says merely, "The thing David had done displeased the LORD."

LIFE QUESTION: *Have you ever been caught in the act, like David, and tried to deceive your way out?*

Caught in the Act

All over the globe today, people who live under the thumb of tyrants ask the question, Who holds the ruler accountable? From the beginning, God had established Israel as *his* kingdom, with its ruler as his representative, not the final authority. And after David's great sin, God sent the prophet Nathan to confront the king.

It was Nathan who had conveyed to the king God's lavish promise to establish David's "house" (1 Chronicles 17). This time he came with a heartrending tale of poverty, greed, and injustice. He presented the case to David, the highest judge in Israel, for a verdict. David knew exactly how to decide such a case: The man deserved to die! When he said so, Nathan delivered his own devastating verdict, "You are the man!"

In this dramatic scene David's greatness shows itself. He could have had Nathan killed or thrown him out of the palace. Instead, he said to Nathan, "I have sinned against the LORD," immediately admitting guilt and acknowledging God as the true ruler.

To appreciate David's confession, you only have to think of the response of leaders "caught in the act" in our own time: a parade of officials marching before the Senate during the Irangate hearings with alibis, excuses, and rationalizations; a presidential candidate denying well-subtantiated charges of habitual womanizing. But King David saw at once the heart of the issue. He had sinned not just against Uriah and his country, but against the Lord.

David was a great king partly because he did not act with the normal pride of a great king. Confronted with the truth, he repented. Forgiveness came in an instant, but the consequences of David's actions would plague the kingdom for a generation. For one thing, he has lost moral authority within his own family. Over the next few years, one of David's sons would rape his sister, and another would kill his brother and launch a coup against David himself. King David had left a legacy of abuse of power, and not all his successors would be so quick to repent.

LIFE QUESTION: *How do you act instinctively when someone confronts you over wrongdoing?*

True Confession

This poem of remembrance may well be the most impressive outcome of David's sordid affair with Bathsheba. It is one thing for a king to confess a moral lapse in private to a prophet. It is quite another for him to compose a detailed account of that confession that could be sung throughout the land!

All nations have heroes, but Israel may be alone in making epic literature about its greatest hero's failings. This eloquent psalm, possibly used in worship services as a guide for confession, shows that Israel ultimately remembered David more for his devotion to God than for his political achievements.

Step by step, the psalm takes the reader (or singer) through the stages of repentance. It describes the constant mental replays—"Oh, if only I had a chance to do it over"—the gnawing guilt, the shame, and finally the hope for a new beginning that springs from true repentance.

David lived under Old Testament law, which prescribed a harsh punishment for his crimes: death by stoning. But in a remarkable way this psalm transcends the rigid formulas of law and reveals the true nature of sin as a broken *relationship* with God. "Against you, you only, have I sinned," David cried out. He could see that no ritual sacrifices or religious ceremonies would cause his guilt to vanish; the sacrifices God wanted were "a broken spirit, a broken and contrite heart." Those, David had.

In the midst of his prayer, David looks for possible good that might come out of his tragedy, and sees a glimmer of light. He prays for God to use his experience as a moral lesson for others. Perhaps, by reading his story of sin, they might avoid the same pitfalls, or by reading his confession they might gain hope in forgiveness. David's prayer was fully answered and is his greatest legacy as king. The best king of Israel fell the farthest. But neither he, nor anyone, can fall beyond the reach of God's love and forgiveness.

LIFE QUESTION: *Would you lose respect for a leader if he or she admitted failures as openly as David did?*

David's Spiritual Secret

KEY VERSE: *O LORD, you have searched me and you know me. You know when I sit and when I rise; you perceive my thoughts from afar. (Ps. 139:1–2)*

*I*n the end, David—lusty, vengeful King David—gained a reputation as a friend of God. For a time in Israel, Jehovah (or Yahweh) was known as "the God of David"; the two were that closely identified. What was David's secret? This majestic psalm hints at an answer.

The psalms form a record of David's conscious effort to subject his own daily life to the reality of that spiritual world beyond him. Mainly, Psalm 139 reveals the *intimacy* that existed between David and his God. Although his exploits—killing wild animals bare-handed, felling Goliath, surviving Saul's onslaughts—made him a hero in his nation's eyes, David always found a way to make God the one on center stage.

Whatever the phrase "practicing the presence of God" means, David experienced it. He intentionally involved God in every detail of his life.

David firmly believed he *mattered* to God. After one narrow escape he wrote, "[God] rescued me because he delighted in me" (Psalm 18:19). Another time he argued, in so many words (Psalm 30), "What good will it do you if I die, Lord? Who will praise you then?" And this psalm, 139, beautifully expresses David's sense of wonder at God's love and concern.

Reading David's psalms, with all their emotional peaks and valleys, it may even seem that he wrote them as a form of spiritual therapy, a way of talking himself into faith when his spirit and emotions were wavering. Now, centuries later, we can use those very same prayers as steps of faith, a path to lead us from an obsession with ourselves to the actual presence of God.

LIFE QUESTION: *How do you "practice the presence of God" in your life?*

The Man Who Had Everything

The first half of 1 Kings describes a man who got life handed to him on a silver platter. The favored son of King David and Queen Bathsheba, young Solomon grew up in the royal palace. Early on, the precocious prince astounded others with his talent for songwriting and natural history.

Even God lavished special gifts on Solomon. In an incredible dream sequence, Solomon actually got the opportunity every child secretly longs for. God offered him any wish—long life, riches, anything at all—and when Solomon chose wisdom, God added bonus gifts of wealth, honor, and peace.

A mere teenager when he took over the throne of Israel, Solomon soon became the richest, most impressive ruler of his time. In Jerusalem, silver was as common as stones (10:27). And a fleet of trading ships brought exotica for the king's private collections—apes and baboons from Africa, and ivory and gold by the ton. He was called the wisest man in the world, and kings and queens traveled hundreds of miles to meet him. They left dazzled by the genius of Israel's king and by the prosperity of his nation.

Israel reached its Golden Age under King Solomon, a shining moment of tranquillity in its long, tormented history. Almost all the Promised Land lay in Solomon's domain, and the nation was at peace. Literature and culture flourished. Of the common people, the Bible reports simply that "they ate, they drank and they were happy" (4:20).

However, even in these happy days, danger signs can be seen. The first verse tells of a shrewd political alliance with Pharoah of Egypt. In addition, Solomon had a passion for foreign-born wives. Over time he married princesses from Moab, Ammon, Edom, Sidon, and other nations—seven hundred wives in all, and three hundred concubines. Eventually, to please his wives, Solomon would take a final, terrible step of building altars to all their gods.

LIFE QUESTION: *Think of people you know who have many natural abilities—do they tend to use those gifts to serve God?*

High-water Mark

Of Solomon's many accomplishments, one looms large above the rest. He spared no expense in building a place for God to indwell, and Solomon's temple, fashioned by 200,000 workmen, soon ranked as one of the wonders of the world. From a distance, it shone like a snowcapped mountain. Inside, the walls and even the floors were plated with pure gold.

In many ways the scene in this chapter represents the high-water mark of the entire Old Testament, the fulfillment of God's covenant with Israel. Solomon called the nation together to dedicate the temple to God, and as thousands of people looked on in a huge public ceremony, the glory of the Lord came down to fill the temple. Even the priests were driven back by the mighty force.

God was making Solomon's temple the center of his activity on earth, and the crowd spontaneously decided to stay another two weeks to celebrate. Kneeling on a bronze platform, Solomon prayed aloud, "I have indeed built a magnificent temple for you, a place for you to dwell forever." Then he caught himself in astonishment. "But will God really dwell on earth? The heavens, even the highest heaven, cannot contain you. How much less this temple I have built!"

God had done it! His promises to Abraham and Moses had finally come true. In one of the most magnificent prayers ever prayed, Solomon reviewed the history of the covenant, and asked God to seal that agreement with his Presence in the temple. God responded: "I have heard the prayer and plea you have made before me; I have consecrated this temple . . . my eyes and my heart will always be there" (9:3).

The Israelites now had land, a nation with secure boundaries, and a gleaming symbol of God's presence among them. All this came to pass in a land rich with silver and gold. On the famous day of the temple dedication, everyone saw the fire and the cloud of his Presence. No one could doubt God's faithfulness.

LIFE QUESTION: *What promises has God kept for you?*

More Than a Building

KEY VERSE:
How lovely is your dwelling place, O LORD Almighty! My soul yearns, even faints, for the courts of the LORD; my heart and my flesh cry out for the living God. (Ps. 84:1–2)

It is almost impossible to exaggerate the significance of the temple for Jews throughout history. They took pride in its beautiful architecture (as people today might honor the Notre Dame cathedral), but the temple was far more than a grand symbol. Israel's entire national religious life centered around this building, the house of God.

Faithful Jews turned and faced the temple daily in prayer. Each year they made pilgrimages there to celebrate three great festivals honoring God's covenant with them. The Israelites even came to believe that the temple magically protected them against foreign invasion. As long as the temple stood, some said, no foreign armies could enter Jerusalem—a belief the prophet Jeremiah soundly condemned.

This psalm captures some of the intense feelings about the temple. It was written by one of the "Sons of Korah," a priestly choir established by King David to provide music for worship. As the writer travels to the temple on pilgrimage, his joy and anticipation make the desert surroundings seem almost like an oasis. Perhaps using a little humor, he claims to envy the sparrows and swallows that build nests inside the walls of the temple and thus get to live there permanently. He sings, "Better is one day in your courts than a thousand elsewhere."

The object of the psalmist's enthusiasm, the glorious temple built by Solomon, stood for about 380 years, occasionally falling into disrepair. Destroyed by the Babylonians, it was rebuilt just before the time of Ezra and Nehemiah, and then reconstructed by King Herod in Jesus' time. Jesus, who also made pilgrimages to the temple, walked in the temple on "Solomon's Porch," and the early church met on the temple grounds.

Herod's temple eventually fell to the Romans, and years later the Moslems built a mosque on the site. But the temple has never lost its sacred significance for the Jews, and even today some in Israel propose rebuilding the temple.

LIFE QUESTION: *Is the worship of God dull or exciting for you? Why? What religious symbols have intense meaning for you?*

Life Advice

KEY VERSE: *Listen, my sons, to a father's instruction; pay attention and gain understanding. . . . Do not set foot on the path of the wicked or walk in the way of evil men. (Prov. 4:1, 14)*

The happy days of Solomon's reign did not last. In a pointed editorial aside, the author of 1 Kings notes that after building the temple Solomon spent twice as much time and energy on the construction of his own palace (7:1). He proved unable to control his extravagant appetite in any area: wealth, power, romance, political intrigue. He seemed obsessed with a desire to outdo anyone who had ever lived, and gradually his devotion to God slipped away. First Kings gives this summation of Solomon's days, "So Solomon did evil in the eyes of the LORD; he did not follow the LORD completely, as David his father had done" (11:6).

Yet, although Solomon ultimately failed to please God, he did use his enormous talent for much good. In the arts, he created many fine works, among them several books of biblical literature. Inspired by God's supernatural gift of wisdom, he composed 1,005 songs and 3,000 proverbs—many of which are collected in this book.

This representative chapter captures the pattern of the book of Proverbs: A wise old man, surrounded by eager young admirers, coyly unveils to them the secrets of his life. (A modern parallel: Millions of Americans will buy the latest how-to book by a famous sports figure or business executive—*maybe it will help me achieve that same kind of success*, they think.) Before revealing his secrets, however, the author of Proverbs wants to get one thing straight. The wisdom he is teaching cannot be reduced to a series of "Don't do this; do that" rules. There is no formula for "one-minute wisdom"; true wisdom demands a lifelong quest. The rewards of such a life, however, will repay any sacrifice, "though it cost all you have."

As the author contrasts "the path of the righteous" with "the way of the wicked," one cannot help wondering how Solomon might have fared if he had consistently followed his own advice. Now, his time passing; he could only hope to convey that hard-bitten wisdom to future generations.

LIFE QUESTION: *Do people today pursue "wisdom" with as much desire and energy? Where do people in modern times pursue "wisdom"?*

How to Read Proverbs

Solomon had the ability to express his great wisdom in a very down-to-earth way. As a result, the book of Proverbs reads like a collection of folksy, common-sense advice. The practical guidance, intended to help you make your way in the world, skips from topic to topic. It comments on small issues as well as large: blabbermouthing, wearing out your welcome with neighbors, being unbearably cheerful too early in the morning.

Anybody can find exceptions to the generalities in Proverbs. For instance, Proverbs 10:4 says "Lazy hands make a man poor, but diligent hands bring wealth." Yet, farmers who work diligently may go hungry during a drought, and lazy dreamers sometimes hit the lottery jackpot. Proverbs simply tells how life works most of the time; it gives the rule, not the exceptions. Normally, people who are godly, moral, hardworking, and wise will succeed in life. Fools and scoffers, though they appear successful, will pay a long-term price for their lifestyles.

The advice in Proverbs usually takes the form of a brief, pungent "one-liner," so the book requires a different kind of reading than others in the Bible. It's hard to read several chapters in a row. The proverbs are meant to be taken in small doses, savored, digested, and gradually absorbed.

Many proverbs are written in a style called "parallelism," a word that describes the tendency of Hebrew poetry to repeat a thought in a slightly different way. One form is "synonymous parallelism," when the second half of the proverb underscores and embellishes the message of the first half (10:10). Another form is "antithetical parallelism," in which a thought is followed by its opposite. In both kinds of parallelism, the trick is to compare each phrase with its pair in the other half of the proverb. For instance, in 10:4 "diligent hands" pairs with its opposite, "lazy hands," and "bring wealth" is the opposite of "make a man poor." Sometimes these comparisons bare subtle shades of meaning.

LIFE QUESTION: *Which of the proverbs in this chapter apply most directly to you?*

Words About Words

*W*ho is the wisest person you know? Probably you'll come up with an elderly person, full of life experience, with a wry twist of humor and a colorful way of putting things. Solomon must have been like that, and he passed down his observations about life in elegant, witty nuggets of insight.

Yet for all its wisdom, Proverbs may well be the most abused book in the Bible. People often quote the proverbs as if they were absolute promises from God or rigid rules for living, when in fact few of them should be read that way. It's best to study the whole book to get its overall point of view on a subject.

Solomon did not sit around all day spouting proverbs in topical sequence. Most likely, those that survive in this book were assembled late in his life, in no strict order. Thus reading Proverbs may at first remind you of reading the dictionary: You'll encounter short, self-contained items in a long list with little or no connection between them.

Even though the one-liners in Proverbs move quickly (and apparently randomly) from one subject to another, there is an overall objective behind the disorder. If you spend enough time in Proverbs, you will gain a subtle and practical understanding of life. Familiar themes keep showing up: the use and abuse of the tongue, wealth and poverty, keeping and losing one's temper, laziness and hard work.

In a "bird's-eye view" survey of the Bible, there is no time for such topical in-depth study. However, the following sampler of proverbs, all dealing with the power of words, shows how such a study might work. Taken together, these proverbs present a wise, balanced view of conversation. They reveal the explosive power—for good or for evil—of ordinary words.

Proverbs on the importance of words: 10:11, 20; 12:14; 15:4; 17:10; 18:21; 25:11. *Proverbs on the wrong way to speak:* 6:16–19; 11:9, 12–13; 12:18; 13:3; 16:27–28; 18:8, 13; 26:23–28; 29:5. *Proverbs on the dangers of words:* 10:19; 14:23.

LIFE QUESTION: *Have you said anything recently that you wish you could unsay?*

Uncommon Song

KEY VERSE: *Like a lily among thorns is my darling among the maidens. Like an apple tree among the trees of the forest is my lover among the young men. (Song 2:2–3)*

*W*ithout doubt more songs have been written about romantic love than any other subject. If you question that, just tune your radio to any popular station and listen for fifteen minutes. You'll hear songs about new love, failed love, wild and crazy love, every kind of love. And, to many people's surprise, the Bible itself contains an explicit love song—complete with erotic lyrics.

Solomon, with all his wives and mistresses, was a devoted student of romance. Ultimately, he fell victim to an obsession with it that caused him much grief. But the Song of Songs (also known as the Song of Solomon) celebrates a high form of beautiful love. It shows no embarrassment about lovers enjoying each other's bodies and openly expressing that enjoyment.

Not everyone has felt comfortable with the frankness of this book. In medieval Spain, Saint Teresa of Avila led a campaign to remove all copies of Song of Songs from the Bible and burn them in public bonfires. Priests and teachers who refused were removed from their jobs, and even imprisoned.

Over the centuries, many others have tried to read the song as though it had nothing to do with physical lovers, seeing it instead as an allegory of love between God and his people. But nowadays most scholars believe that the poem was intended to be taken at face value, as a celebration of love between a newly-married couple.

These lovers look without shame on one another, and tell each other what they feel. They revel in the sensuous: the beauty of nature, the scent of perfumes and spices. They are explicit and erotic. Yet, Song of Songs creates a very different atmosphere than most modern love songs. It harks back to the original love in the Garden of Eden, when man and woman were naked and unashamed. You sense no shame or guilt; you feel that God himself smiles upon their love.

LIFE QUESTION: *What similarities do you see between this chapter and modern love songs? What differences?*

Dangling

KEY VERSE: *I have seen the burden God has laid on men. He has made everything beautiful in its time. He has also set eternity in the hearts of men; yet they cannot fathom what God has done from beginning to end. (Eccl. 3:10–11)*

*P*eople surprised to find a book like Song of Songs in the Bible may be knocked flat by the book of Ecclesiastes. "Meaningless! Meaningless! Everything is meaningless!" cries the author of this bleak capitulation of despair.

Although Ecclesiastes mentions no author by name, it contains broad hints that King Solomon was, if not its author, then at least its inspiration. It tells the story of the richest, wisest, most famous man in the world, who follows every pleasure impulse as far as it can lead him. This man, "the Teacher," finally collapses in regret and despair; he has squandered his life.

This early chapter gives a capsule summary, beginning with an elegant poem about Time and proceeding from there into musings about life typical of the Teacher's search for meaning. The author concludes that God has laid a "burden" on humanity that keeps us from finding ultimate satisfaction on earth. After a lifetime spent in the pursuit of pleasure, the Teacher was driven to ask, "Is that all there is?" Even the rare moments of peace and satisfaction he had found were easily spoiled by the onrushing threat of death. According to the Teacher, life doesn't make sense outside of God and will, in fact, never fully make sense because we are not God.

But God has also "set eternity in the hearts of men." We feel longings for something more: pleasures that will last forever; love that won't go sour; fulfillment, not boredom, from our work.

The Teacher thus dangles between two states, feeling a steady drag toward despair but also a tug toward something higher. Much like a personal journal, the book of Ecclesiastes records his search for balance. The tension does not resolve in this chapter, and some readers wonder if it resolves at all. But Ecclesiastes ends with one final word of advice, the summation of all the Teacher's wisdom: "Fear God and keep his commandments, for this is the whole duty of man" (12:13).

LIFE QUESTION: *The Teacher is painfully honest about his doubts and despair. What portions of this chapter did you especially identify with?*

The Northern Kingdom

New Breed of Heroes

KEY VERSE:
Then the woman said to Elijah, "Now I know that you are a man of God and that the word of the LORD from your mouth is the truth."
(1 Kings 17:24)

*I*n the end, Solomon's weaknesses seriously eroded the kingdom of Israel. His lavish public projects laid a heavy tax burden on its citizens and forced him to conscript some of them as virtual slaves. His moral failures undermined the spiritual unity of the nation, and the brief, shining vision of a covenant nation gradually faded away. After Solomon's death, the nation split in two and slid toward ruin.

The remaining part of the Old Testament can prove especially confusing: the two nations had thirty-nine rulers between them, and a couple dozen prophets besides. To avoid getting hopelessly lost, keep these basic facts in mind: *Israel* was the breakaway Northern Kingdom, with a capital city of Samaria. All its rulers proved unfaithful to God. *Judah* was the Southern Kingdom, with its capital in Jerusalem. In general its rulers, descendants of David, remained more faithful to God and his covenant, and consequently Judah survived 136 years longer.

Although the Bible discusses all thirty-nine rulers by name, after Solomon stories of the kings speed up into a forgettable blur. God turns instead to his prophets.

Elijah, the wildest and wooliest prophet of all, first makes an appearance in this chapter. He illustrates better than anyone else the decisive change: where King Solomon had worn jewelry and fine clothes and lived luxuriously in a gilded palace, Elijah wore a diaper-like covering of black camel's hair, slept in the wilderness, and had to beg—or pray—for handouts. He came on the scene when Israel was thriving politically, but floundering spiritually. Queen Jezebel had just launched a campaign to murder all true prophets of God and replace them with a thousand pagan priests.

This chapter shows glimpses of Elijah during his fugitive days. Although he was a moody prophet, subject to bouts of depression and self-doubt, he clearly had God on his side. The salvation of Israel would depend on how well they listened to prophets like Elijah.

LIFE QUESTION: *What do you learn about Elijah's personality in this chapter?*

Mountaintop Showdown

Mountaintop Showdown

KEY VERSE: *Then Elijah said, . . . "you call on the name of your god, and I will call on the name of the LORD. The god who answers by fire—he is God." (1 Kings 18:22–24)*

In ancient Africa, tribes would sometimes fight their battles single-combat style. Great armies lined up across from each other, waving their weapons menacingly and hurling insults back and forth. When tribal hatred reached a kind of critical mass, two warriors—only two—stepped forward to fight on behalf of all the rest. Whoever drew first blood would prove the gods were on his side, and his opponent's army would surrender. Something like single-combat warfare took place at a moment of deep crisis in Israel. As usual, the prophet Elijah was on center stage.

Elijah journeyed across Israel to a rugged mountain to confront his pagan enemies. Few scenes in history can match the one that transpired on windswept Mount Carmel. On one side stood a resplendent array of 850 prophets of Baal and Asherah; on the other stood a lone, bedraggled desert prophet of God. Elijah let the pagan prophets have first turn. As they danced around an altar beseeching their gods, he sat back and taunted them to frenzy. "Maybe your god is traveling, or sleeping," he yelled, and the priests slashed themselves with swords until the blood ran.

Elijah may have been outnumbered, but he proved a worthy adversary. When his time came, he worked the crowd like a master magician. He stacked the odds against a miracle by dousing the site with twelve large jars of water—the most precious commodity in Israel after a three-year drought. Just when it seemed Elijah was perpetrating a huge national joke, the miracle happened: fire fell from heaven. The crowd dropped to the ground in fear and awe. The heat was enough to melt even the stones and soil, and flames licked water from the trenches as if it were fuel.

Elijah's very name meant "The LORD is my God," and, in the final analysis, the showdown on Mount Carmel was no contest at all. Elijah went on to orchestrate one of the greatest outbreaks of miracles in biblical history. It was as if God was sounding a loud, unmistakable final warning to the North—a warning they failed to heed.

LIFE QUESTION: *This chapter shows God revealing himself in a spectacular public display. Have you known him to do such things today?*

A Worthy Replacement

KEY VERSE: *When Elisha the man of God heard that the king of Israel had torn his robes, he sent him this message: "Why have you torn your robes? Have the man come to me and he will know that there is a prophet in Israel." (2 Kings 5:8)*

*W*ho could replace a mighty prophet like Elijah? When the time came to choose a successor, Elijah settled on his most faithful companion, a farmer named Elisha. While Elijah was a loner, often a fugitive, and preached a stern message of judgment, Elisha lived among common people, and stressed life, hope, and God's grace.

Elisha lived a colorful life: He led a school of prophets, served as a military spy, advised kings, and even anointed revolutionaries. Easily recognizable with his bald head and wooden walking staff, he became a famous figure in Israel, especially as reports of his miracles spread. Elisha had asked for a double portion of Elijah's spirit, and the Bible pointedly records about twice as many miracles performed by Elisha. Many of these miracles prefigure the miracles Jesus himself would later perform; they show God caring for the needs of poor and outcast people.

In this chapter Elisha is seen offering assistance to a high-ranking enemy general. Naaman's pilgrimage shows how far Elisha's fame had spread. A pagan king was willing to seek help from God's prophet in order to get a general's health restored.

Elisha's brusque treatment of generals and kings contrasts sharply with the tenderness he showed toward the poor and oppressed. The bizarre procedure he prescribed, along with his refusal to take payment, offended Naaman. Elisha, however, was making it clear that healing came not through magical powers or a shaman's secret technique, but through God—and God required obedience and humility even of five-star generals with piles of gold.

Jesus referred to this story at the beginning of his ministry (Luke 4:27). He made the same point as Elisha: Don't try to "box in" God. He is to be obeyed, on his own terms, not manipulated.

LIFE QUESTION: *One writer has defined the Christian life as "living by God's surprises." Has God ever surprised you?*

The Day the Earth Will Shake

Scenes from the lives of Elijah and Elisha—fire on Mount Carmel, the widow's oil, Naaman's healing, the chariots of fire—are among the most familiar of Old Testament stories. But the prophets who followed them performed few miracles, relying less on spectacular displays of power and more on the power of the Word.

The prophet Joel provides a brief introduction to the style of the writing prophets. No one knows for sure when he delivered his messages—they could have come anywhere within a four-century span. No one is even sure whether he lived in Israel of the North or Judah of the South. But in gripping prose he warned his people of a terrible disaster to come. This chapter captures as well as any the essential message of all the prophets.

A day of judgment. Nearly every prophet begins with words meant to inspire fear and dread. Some warned of invading armies, and some of natural disasters. For example, Joel paints vivid pictures of an army of locusts. The locusts could symbolically represent human armies, but may also be taken literally.

A call to repentence. The prophets raise alarm with good reason, for they see such disasters as a consequence of their nation's unfaithfulness to God. They urgently call on their people to turn from their evil ways. Joel 2:13 could stand as a single, eloquent summary of the heart of the prophets' message.

A future of hope. Every biblical prophet, no matter how dour, gets around to a word of hope. Taken together, they tell of a time when God will make right everything wrong with the earth, a time when The World As It Is will finally match The World As God Wants It.

Joel 2 is a fine capsule summary of this threefold message.

LIFE QUESTION: *Peter applied Joel's prophecy about "the day of the LORD" to the events of Pentecost (Acts 2:17–21). Have all of Joel's prophecies already been fulfilled?*

Beloved Enemies

KEY VERSE: *When God saw what they did and how they turned from their evil ways, he had compassion and did not bring upon them the destruction he had threatened. But Jonah was greatly displeased and became angry. (Jonah 3:10–4:1)*

Nearly everyone knows about the misadventures that befell Jonah on his journey to Nineveh: the ocean storm and the detour in the belly of a whale. But readers of Jonah often miss the central point, the reason for Jonah's misadventures in the first place. He was rebelling against God's mercy. Jonah offers a true-life study of how hard it is to follow the biblical command, "Love your enemies." While many people admire that command, few find it easy to put into practice.

Jonah had understandable reason to balk at God's orders to preach in Nineveh, for that city was the capital of an empire renowned for its cruelty. Assyrian soldiers had no qualms about "scorched earth" military tactics. Typically, after destroying an enemy's fields and cities, they would slaughter the conquered peoples or hammer iron hooks through their noses or lower lips and lead them away as slaves. Jonah wanted no part in giving such bullies a chance to repent. But amazingly, God loved Nineveh and wanted to save the city, not destroy it. He knew the people were ripe for change.

The book of Jonah powerfully expresses God's yearning to forgive, and these two brief chapters fill in the lesser-known details of Jonah's mission. To the prophet's disgust, a simple announcement of doom sparked a spiritual revival in pagan Nineveh. And Jonah, sulking under a shriveled vine, admitted he had suspected God's soft heart all along. He could not trust God—could not, that is, trust him to be harsh and unrelenting toward Nineveh.

The book also reveals God's ultimate purpose for his chosen people: He wanted them, like Jonah, to reach out to other people and demonstrate his love and forgiveness. Nineveh's wholehearted response put the Israelites to shame, for not once did they respond to a prophet like these Assyrians did.

LIFE QUESTION: *Have you ever consciously tried to love the "enemies" in your life?*

Street-corner Prophet

"I gave you empty stomachs in every city and lack of bread in every town, yet you have not returned to me," declares the LORD. *(Amos 4:6)*

Amos appeared on the scene when Israel, the Northern Kingdom, was booming. They had beaten back all their traditional enemies and even invaded neighboring Judah, taking land and prisoners. For a change, the government was stable: King Jeroboam II presided over a half-century of prosperity and strength. People were too busy enjoying the good life to listen to the rantings of a prophet, and for precisely that reason Amos spoke in italics and exclamation points.

Unlike Jonah, Amos was not a professional prophet. He was a man of the land, a shepherd and a tender of sycamore trees. A migrant to Israel from the South, he spoke with a rural accent and was probably the butt of many jokes by city sophisticates.

Amos the peasant could not get over what he found in the Northern cities. The luxurious lifestyles shocked him: gorgeous couches, beds of carved ivory, summer homes, top-grade meat, fine wine. It seemed obvious to Amos that this extravagance was built on a foundation of injustice: oppression of the poor, dishonest business practices, court bribes, privilege bought with money.

Lulled into security by their powerful, victorious army, the Israelites thought they were safe for generations. But, as Amos warned, Israel could not forever push God into a small corner of their lives, to be brought out like a magic charm whenever they needed him.

"Prepare to meet your God, O Israel," Amos shouted from the street corners, but those words had about as much impact in his day as they do in ours. Nevertheless, the prophet's warnings proved true: in a remarkably short time, Israel fell apart. A mere thirty years after Jeroboam II's reign, the Northern Kingdom of Israel ceased to exist.

Amos is not a comfortable book to read—its message hits too close to our own time, when nations judge success by the size of gross national product and military forces. For that reason alone, it deserves a close look.

LIFE QUESTION: *What parallels do you see between Amos's time and our own?*

Human Object Lesson

KEY VERSE: *The LORD said to me, "Go, show your love to your wife again, though she is loved by another and is an adulteress. Love her as the LORD loves the Israelites, though they turn to other gods." (Hos. 3:1)*

Just a few years after Amos, as Israel was breaking apart and sliding toward chaos, a word from God came to Hosea. To a shattered nation, Hosea brought a hope-filled message of grace and forgiveness.

Most books of the prophets focus on the audience and all the things they've done wrong. Hosea, in contrast, shines the spotlight on God. What is it like to be God? How must he feel when his chosen people reject him and go panting after false gods? As if words alone were too weak to convey his passion, God asked Hosea to act out a living parable. He married a loose woman named Gomer, who soon ran away and committed adultery. Only by living out that drama could Hosea understand, and then express, something of how Israel's rebuke felt to God.

After all that Gomer had done, God instructed Hosea simply to invite her back and forgive her. The pattern hopelessly repeated itself. Gomer bore two children—but was Hosea really their father? According to the Mosaic Law, he should have turned his adulterous wife out on the street, or had her tried in court. What Hosea did, and God did, was unheard of.

Hosea is one of the most emotional books in the Bible, an outpouring of suffering love from God's heart. Read aloud, this chapter sounds like a fight between a husband wife overheard through thin walls. The book of Hosea, in fact, represents the first time God's covenant with Israel was described in terms of marriage. It shows that God longs for his people with the tenderness and hunger that a lover feels toward his bride.

In the covenant, Israel had agreed to love and obey God no matter what, "till death do us part." But as they prospered in the new land, that flame of love died. The old covenant was fractured. As Hosea tells it, the death of their love broke God's heart. God could only promise another chance, with a new covenant at a future time when "you will call me 'my husband'; you will no longer call me 'my master.'"

LIFE QUESTION: *Hosea describes various stages in Israel's relationship to God. What stage are you in with God?*

Wounded Lover

KEY VERSE:

"When Israel was a child, I loved him, and out of Egypt I called my son. But the more I called Israel, the further they went from me." (Hos. 11:1–2)

Many people carry around the image of God as an impersonal Force, something akin to the law of gravity. Hosea portrays almost the opposite: a God of passion and fury and tears and love. A God in mourning over Israel's rejection of him.

God used Hosea's unhappy story to illustrate his own whipsaw emotions. That first blush of love when he found Israel, he said, was like finding grapes in the desert. But as Israel broke his trust again and again, he had to endure the awful shame of a wounded lover. God's words carry a tone surprisingly like self-pity: "I am like a moth to Ephraim, like rot to the people of Judah" (5:12).

The powerful image of a jilted lover explains why, in a chapter like Hosea 11, God's emotions seem to vacillate so. He is preparing to obliterate Israel—wait, now he is weeping, holding out open arms—no, he is sternly pronouncing judgment again. Those shifting moods seem hopelessly irrational, except to anyone who has been jilted by a lover.

Is there a more powerful human feeling than that of betrayal? Ask a high school girl whose boyfriend has just dumped her for a pretty cheerleader. Or tune your radio to a country-western station and listen to the lyrics of infidelity. Or check out the murders reported in the daily newspaper; an amazing proportion trace back to a fight with an estranged lover. Hosea, and God, demonstrate in living color exactly what it is like to love someone desperately, and get nothing in return. Not even God, with all his power, can force a human being to love him.

Virtually every chapter of Hosea talks about the "prostitution" or "adultery" of God's people. God the lover will not share his bride with anyone else. Yet, amazingly, even when she turns her back on him, he sticks with her. He is willing to suffer, in hope that someday she will change. Hosea proves that God longs not to punish, but to love.

LIFE QUESTION: *What is your strongest memory of feeling betrayed?*

Postmortem

An impressive lineup of prophets all tried their hand at convincing Israel to change its ways. But neither the miracles of Elijah and Elisha nor the shouts of Amos nor the impassioned pleas of Hosea had much effect. When times of trouble came, the nation turned toward foreign gods and frantically signed up military allies; they never turned wholeheartedly to God.

The day of judgment so harrowingly foretold by the prophets is here recorded in the flat, matter-of-fact language of history. The end for the Northern Kingdom of Israel came when Israel's kings, against all the prophets' advice, sought to purchase political protection, first from Assyria, and then from Egypt. Discovering the double cross, Assyria sent an army against Israel.

In early wars Assyrian conquerors had exterminated their enemies, but in later years they adopted the new technique of deporting their victims and replacing them with foreigners from other conquered territories. The radical disruption of their societies tended to keep conquered peoples from regrouping and rising up as a new threat. In keeping with that policy, Assyria deported 27,290 captives from the land of Israel, dispersing the "ten lost tribes of Israel."

These emigrés the Assyrians replaced with foreigners who formed a new identity as "Samaritans," a group that existed in New Testament times and, in fact, can still be found in modern Israel. Samaritan settlers combined their native religions with some reverence for the true God.

After this chapter, the Bible's attention turns south toward Judah, the collective name for the two surviving tribes of Israelites. Why did the Assyrian tragedy happen? Second Kings diagnoses idolatry as the chief cause of Israel's moral collapse. Ominously, the practice had already gained a foothold in the Southern Kingdom as well.

LIFE QUESTION: *Why do you think God viewed idolatry as such a serious crime?*

The Southern Kingdom

Meanwhile in Jerusalem

So far our readings have sampled the 200-year history of Israel, which began sliding away from God from the very first days of its birth as a nation. But the Bible devotes far more space to the kings and prophets of the Southern Kingdom. Of the nineteen men and one woman who ruled Judah, at least a handful demonstrated a quality of spiritual leadership unmatched in the Northern Kingdom. Judah proved more faithful in living up to the covenant with God, and chiefly for that reason it outlasted Israel by nearly a century and a half.

This chapter tells of the extraordinary king named Jehoshaphat, one of Judah's early rulers. No ruler of Judah had a wholly peaceful reign, and as a result much of the action in 2 Chronicles takes place, like this story, on a battlefield. Here is the book's philosophy of war in a nutshell: *If you trust in your own military might or that of powerful neighbors, you will lose. Instead, humble yourself and rely totally on God—regardless of the odds against you.*

As the kings of Judah demonstrated with monotonous regularity, it took uncommon courage to rely on God alone at a moment of great peril. Even the best of them dipped into the royal treasury to purchase help from neighboring allies. But King Jehoshaphat provides a textbook example of the proper response. When invading armies threatened, he called the entire nation together in a giant prayer meeting. On the day of battle, he sent a choir in front of his army to sing praises to God.

Jehoshaphat's tactics may seem more suitable for a summer camp meeting than a battlefield, but they worked. The enemy forces all turned against each other, and Judah's army marched home victorious.

This bright moment of national faith shines out from a very mottled historical record. By his public prayer and personal example, King Jehoshaphat showed what could happen when a leader placed complete trust in God.

LIFE QUESTION: *Have any modern leaders demonstrated inspiring faith?*

Rumors of Destruction

Not every king of Judah had Jehoshaphat's faith and courage. As the years ground on, the same decadence that had characterized the Northern Kingdom of Israel spread like an epidemic through Judah. Other parts of the Bible detail Judah's faults: one notorious king, Ahaz, set up foreign altars, offered his own children in human sacrifice, and shuttered the Lord's temple. Along with the religious corruption came every other kind of sin: dishonesty, greed, bribery, injustice.

Around the same time Amos was blasting Israel in the North, another country preacher, Micah, was called by God to deliver similar words of warning to Judah. Micah, a prophet who got emotionally caught up in his message, lived in tumultuous times. Once, Judah lost 120,000 soldiers in a single day (2 Chronicles 28:6). The nation watched in fear as Assyria, the chief power of the day, brutally smashed the Northern Kingdom. What would keep Judah from a similar fate? That very prospect of judgment was what made Micah howl like a jackal and moan like an owl.

This chapter opens with an impassioned plea from God. "My people, what have I done to you?" God asks. He reviews the history of his chosen people, reminding them of his great works on their behalf. In his rhetorical response, Micah makes clear that God desires true, heartfelt changes, not just a veneer of religion.

Micah concludes darkly that his people, afflicted with the same sickness as their relatives to the North, would meet the same end. Even so, Micah saw light ahead. Amid graphic predictions of destruction, Micah gives clear predictions of the Messiah, the future leader from the tiny town of Bethlehem who would offer new hope to the earth (5:2).

LIFE QUESTION: *Imagine God personally addressing your church, spelling out exactly what changes he wants. What would he say?*

Happy Days Are Here Again

Toward the end of Micah's career, just as the situation in Judah was deteriorating, another great king took the throne. In fact, 2 Chronicles spends more time on Hezekiah than on anyone else. The very first year of his reign he led a program to restore the temple, which had fallen into disrepair from lack of use. Hezekiah turned the tables on Judah's priests: He stood in the temple square and delivered a rousing sermon to *them*.

When Hezekiah decided to sponsor a huge religious festival, the idea at first met with scorn and ridicule. But a king's proclamation carries certain weight, and the nation finally did come together in a remarkable scene of happiness and unity. Hezekiah even sent "missionary" couriers to the devastated land to the North, and some survivors of the Assyrian scourge made their way to Jerusalem.

This chapter closely resembles 1 Kings 8 and its story of Solomon's dedication of the temple. Hezekiah was intent on renewing the covenant with God in hopes of forestalling God's judgment. The details of the festival celebration show just how badly Judah had neglected the covenant: There was a shortage of priests, and Hezekiah had to bend the rules or not enough worshipers would have been properly purified.

It was no accident that Hezekiah organized his festival around the Passover. That day marked the birth of a nation, when God freed his people from slavery in Egypt. In a real sense, the Passover had sealed the covenant, and Hezekiah determined to remind the nation of its heritage.

Despite the initial skepticism, the people of Judah got caught up in the celebration and, as in Solomon's day, spontaneously decided to stay another seven days. "There was great joy in Jerusalem," the Bible reports, "for since the days of Solomon son of David king of Israel there had been nothing like this in Jerusalem."

LIFE QUESTION: *When you hear about a religious renewal or "revival," do you tend to be skeptical, cautious, open-minded, enthusiastic?*

Power Behind the Throne

KEY VERSE: *Then I heard the voice of the Lord saying, "Whom shall I send? And who will go for us?" And I said, "Here am I. Send me!" (Isa. 6:8)*

This chapter flashes back to a scene that took place two decades before Hezekiah became king. The prophet Isaiah, a giant of Jewish history, received a direct, dramatic call from God.

When Isaiah began his work, Judah seemed strong and wealthy. But Isaiah saw signs of grave danger—the very same signs that had alarmed his contemporary, the prophet Micah. Men went around drunk; women cared more about their clothes than about their neighbors' hunger. People gave lip service to God and kept up the outward appearance of religion, but little more.

External dangers loomed even larger: on all sides monster empires were burgeoning. The nation of Judah, said Isaiah, stood at a crossroads. It could either regain its footing or begin a perilous slide downward.

Two kings, Jotham and Ahaz, paid Isaiah little heed. But, in a remarkable turnaround, the new king Hezekiah made Isaiah one of his most trusted advisers. In any moment of crisis, he called upon the prophet.

Not every prophet blasted the establishment from street corners. Isaiah spent his days in the corridors of power, offering political advice and helping set the course of his nation. Although he sometimes stood alone against a crowd of contrary advisers, he never tempered his message. Isaiah outlasted four kings, but he finally offended one beyond repair. Tradition records that the last, King Manasseh, had Isaiah killed by fastening him between two planks of wood and sawing his body in half.

It seems likely that much of Hezekiah's zeal for reform traces back to the influence of the prophet Isaiah. The divine call recorded in this chapter shows where Isaiah got the courage and commitment that made him such an important force in Judah's history.

LIFE QUESTION: *When have you "volunteered" for a difficult task for God?*

Eloquent Hope

KEY VERSE:

In that day they will say, "Surely this is our God; we trusted in him, and he saved us. This is the LORD, we trusted in him; let us rejoice and be glad in his salvation." (Isa. 25:9)

In addition to his role as adviser to kings, Isaiah was a writer of enormous talent. No other biblical author can match his rich vocabulary and use of imagery, and the New Testament quotes him more than all the other prophets combined. Many of his majestic phrases have become part of the English vocabulary.

Using his great ability, Isaiah tried to awaken Judah from its spiritual slump. Like most of the prophets, he preached a two-part message of **judgment** to come unless people radically change their ways; and **hope** in a future when God will restore not only the Israelites, but the whole world.

During the period when Judah was fat, self-indulgent, and reveling in luxury, Isaiah warned of a reckoning day. But later, when Jerusalem was surrounded by foreign troops, Isaiah offered stirring words of hope. World-class tyrants didn't intimidate Isaiah; he knew that God could toss them aside like twigs.

Isaiah summons up latent human longings for a better world. He had no doubt that God will one day transform this pockmarked planet into a new earth that has no tears, no pain, no death. In the future world as pictured by Isaiah, wild animals will lie beside each other in peace. Weapons will be melted into farm tools.

At a given point in history God may appear powerless, or blithely unconcerned about the violence and evil that plague this planet. The people of Jerusalem certainly questioned his concern in the face of the Assyrian invasion. Isaiah gave them a local message of hope: entrust your future to God alone. And he expanded that message to encompass the entire world.

Isaiah 24–27 gives a preview of the end of all history. First will come a difficult time, when God purifies the stained earth. Like a woman in childbirth, the earth will undergo pain and struggle. But what follows next will be a future life so wonderful we can scarcely imagine it.

LIFE QUESTION: *What gives you hope about the future?*

City Under Siege

It was the greatest crisis that Hezekiah and Isaiah ever faced. The very survival of Judah was in peril. Assyria, ever thirsty for more conquests, had just rolled into Judah, leveling forty-six walled cities and taking 200,150 captives. The Assyrian king demanded huge sums of money from Hezekiah, whom he mockingly described as "a bird in a cage." Hezekiah might as well have been in a cage, for siege armies completely surrounded his city.

Cowering behind his city's walls, Hezekiah once more turned to Isaiah for advice. Should he surrender? Negotiate? Outside, the Assyrians were directing a barrage of propaganda at Jerusalem's demoralized citizens. They scoffed at Judah's hopes for a miracle from God. No gods had helped any other nation withstand the Assyrian juggernaut.

Isaiah, however, refused to panic. Against all odds, he calmly advised prayer and reliance on the power of God. *Have faith,* he said. *Don't surrender, and don't fear. Assyria will return home, wounded.*

Jerusalem looked like a doomed city during the siege by Assyria. But two things happened to fulfill Isaiah's prophecy. First, a great plague struck the Assyrians (Isaiah 37), a plague also recorded by the historian Herodotus. Later, the murder of Assyria's leader brought internal chaos to that country and canceled out the Assyrian threat.

The miraculous deliverance saved Judah, but only temporarily. In his latter days, Hezekiah foolishly flaunted his country's wealth before envoys from Babylon, a rising power in the East. The citizens of Judah grew proud as well; they became convinced that Jerusalem, God's city, was indestructible—a belief that would be proven tragically false.

LIFE QUESTION: *Verses 7 and 31 show that God may sometimes seem close, and sometimes distant. What makes the difference?*

Enemy Justice

Nahum had one distinct advantage over most biblical prophets: he was addressing an enemy. The nation of Assyria had just obliterated the Northern Kingdom of Israel and, except for God's miraculous intervention in Hezekiah's day, would have done the same to Nahum's homeland of Judah.

Assyria was an easy enemy to hate—something along the line of Hitler's Germany. Its soldiers decimated cities, led captives away with hooks in their noses, and plowed salt into fertile ground. In fact, Assyria's very obnoxiousness lay at the heart of what Nahum had to say.

A question nagged at Judah's citizens, who had experienced the full force of Assyria's "endless cruelty." Assyria had trampled a huge path of destruction from the region of modern-day Turkey down the Persian Gulf all the way to Egypt. Judah, in contrast, was a tiny vassal state barely clinging to existence. Why would God hold Judah accountable but allow Assyria to go unpunished?

Nahum brashly predicted that even mighty Assyria would meet its end. Its people had repented once, in Jonah's day, but had reverted to old patterns that would bring on God's judgment. Undoubtedly, the people of Judah applauded Nahum's prophecies—but who could believe them? Assyria, the most powerful empire in the world for two hundred years, would not simply disappear.

Nahum delivered these prophecies sometime around 700 B.C. In 612 B.C., Nineveh, the last Assyrian stronghold, fell to the Babylonians and Persians. Over time a carpet of grass covered the pile of rubble marking what had been the greatest city of its time.

Like all the biblical prophets, Nahum saw beyond the intimidating forces of history. He knew that behind the rise and fall of empires an even greater force was at work, determining the ultimate outcome. Though God's justice may seem slow, nothing can finally escape it.

LIFE QUESTION: *What modern-day injustices seem to be going unpunished?*

Rotten Ruling Class

KEY VERSE: *I said to the city, "Surely you will fear me and accept correction!"*. . . *But they were still eager to act corruptly in all they did. (Zeph. 3:7)*

Through the influence of prophets like Micah and Isaiah, King Hezekiah helped set the land of Judah back on course. However, Hezekiah's death unfortunately vacated the throne for Manasseh, who proved to be one of Judah's all-time worst kings. In his fifty-year reign—the longest of any king of Israel or Judah—Manasseh reversed all the good that Hezekiah had accomplished.

An unabashed tyrant, Manasseh filled the streets of Jerusalem with blood. (It was he who, according to tradition, had Isaiah sawn in two.) He made child sacrifice common practice, built astrology altars in God's temple, and encouraged male prostitution as part of religious ritual. By the time he died, very few reminders of the covenant with God remained in Judah. Public shrines abounded, and storefronts in Jerusalem were advertising household gods, mediums, and spiritists. God's chosen people had out-paganized the pagans.

The next king, Amon, started out in his father's footsteps, but this time his own officials rose up in revolt and assassinated him after two years. The nation of Judah, cut loose from its moorings, was drifting toward total anarchy. And Josiah, the pint-size prince crowned by Amon's supporters, hardly gave much reason for optimism.

In the early days of Josiah's reign, the prophet Zephaniah spoke out against the decadence spreading throughout Judah. Other prophets had come from peasant stock; Zephaniah proudly traced his ancestry back to King Hezekiah. Yet, unlike others of high social standing, he didn't try to defend the upper classes. Rather, he accused them of chief responsibility for the decay in Judah. The officials, the priests, the rulers, the judges, even the prophets—these are the targets of Zephaniah's rage.

The leaders of Judah were pointing the entire nation on a course of self-destruction. Unless they reversed directions, Jerusalem would face the same fate as many of its fallen neighbors.

LIFE QUESTION: *Zephaniah begins with gloom but ends with joy. What gives him reason for hope?*

Judah's Boy Wonder

The Bible does not record what specific effect Zephaniah's words had within Judah. But it does give a thrilling account of a turnaround that occurred during his days, led by King Josiah.

King Josiah took over at the age of eight, in the midst of a crisis seemingly beyond all healing. But Josiah was no ordinary eight-year-old. Raised by a wicked king in a wicked time, he somehow emerged with a spiritual vision that had no equal. Against the odds, Josiah steered his nation back toward God.

Josiah devoted much time and energy to a favorite public works project, repairing the temple. And one busy day, as carpenters sawed new joists and beams, and masons carved new stones for the temple walls, and workmen hauled off rubble from the idols Josiah had smashed—in the midst of that din and clutter, a priest made an amazing discovery. He found a scroll that looked like— *could it be?*—the Book of the Covenant, the original record of the agreement between the Israelites and their God. (Most scholars believe the scroll contained part or all of the book of Deuteronomy.)

The neglect of such an important document, long buried and forgotten, shows the extent of Judah's slide away from God. And Josiah's response shows the depth of his commitment. Hearing those sacred words for the first time, he tore his robes in shame and repentance. And after a prophetess had confirmed the scroll's authenticity, Josiah pledged himself and his nation to the terms of the long-lost covenant.

This chapter tells the story of the dramatic discovery, and the next tells of Josiah's fervent campaign to call his nation back to God. His actions would change the landscape of Judah and stave off certain destruction. All this came about because a young king took seriously the words of God.

LIFE QUESTION: *When have you experienced an "awakening" similar to King Josiah's?*

National Adultery

Zephaniah was not the only prophet active during King Josiah's days. Just as Josiah was reaching adulthood, the doleful voice of Jeremiah began to be heard in the streets of Jerusalem. Later, Jeremiah's messages were collected into a book that is the Bible's longest, and easily its most passionate. Jeremiah was subject to violent swings of mood, and his book reflects that same emotional temperament. The English word *jeremiad,* which means "a long complaint," conveys something of his tone.

This chapter, full of strong images and rhetorical blasts, typifies Jeremiah's style. He uses sexual imagery to present Judah's crisis as a kind of lover's quarrel between God and Judah. She is like a prostitute who lies down under every spreading tree; like a rutting she-camel; like a donkey in heat driven wild with desire.

But what is the object of Judah's desire? Incredibly, she is trading the glory of God for worthless idols of wood and stone. God, the wounded lover, cannot comprehend his people's actions, and neither can Jeremiah.

Jeremiah had two main complaints against Judah: She prostituted herself both through idol worship and through alliances with foreign nations. When a military threat loomed, Judah turned to empires like Assyria, Egypt, or Babylon for help, not to God.

Josiah, one of Judah's all-time best kings, led a mostly successful campaign to rid the nation of idols. But even Josiah succumbed to the temptation of foreign entanglements. Against Jeremiah's counsel, he led an ill-advised march against Egyptian armies. Josiah died in that battle, and his death shocked the nation. A grieving Jeremiah wrote laments in honor of the king.

Judah would never recover from Josiah's fatal mistake. Egypt installed a puppet king over Judah, and from then on no one had the ability to rally Judah's religious or political strength. Jeremiah lived through the reigns of four weakling kings, and the messages collected in this book heap scorn upon them.

LIFE QUESTION: *To whom do you show the most consistent loyalty? Are you loyal to God?*

Balky Prophet

KEY VERSE:

I will make you a wall to this people, a fortified wall of bronze; they will fight against you but will not overcome you, for I am with you. (Jer. 15:20)

For most of his life Jeremiah had to deliver a gloomy message, and no one felt the weight of that message more than he. "Since my people are crushed, I am crushed; I mourn, and horror grips me. . . . Oh that my head were a spring of water and my eyes a fountain of tears" (8:21, 9:1). That spirit comes through so strongly in his writings that Jeremiah has become known as "the weeping prophet."

More than Judah's future caused Jeremiah alarm; he feared for his own personal safety. From the very beginning he argued with God about his assignment as a prophet. God made harsh demands on Jeremiah, and he responded to those demands in typical fashion: by whining, complaining, feeling sorry for himself, and even lashing out against God's cruelty. The book includes a remarkable series of conversations—more like arguments—in which Jeremiah tells God exactly how he feels.

This chapter includes one such conversation with God. Quotation marks surround God's speeches: He begins by pronouncing judgment on the nation of Judah. But at verse 10 Jeremiah butts in with his agenda. What will people think of a prophet delivering a message like that? His name is a national swear word already. He'd be better off unborn. God resumes his solemn pronouncement in verse 12, only to be interrupted again by Jeremiah's self-piteous complaints. To him, God seems unreliable, like a brook that dries up, a spring that fails.

Despite Jeremiah's fits and protests, God never gave up on him. He promised to make the weepy prophet "a fortified wall of bronze," able to stand against the whole land. Likewise, Jeremiah, for all his diatribes, never gave up on God. The word of God was inside him and he couldn't stop talking about it. "But if I say, 'I will not mention him or speak any more in his name,' his word is in my heart like a fire, a fire shut up in my bones. I am weary of holding it in; indeed, I cannot."

LIFE QUESTION: _What "complaints" would you bring to God? Do you, like Jeremiah, ever feel unappreciated by God?_

No Dead End

Trained as a priest, Jeremiah learned at an early age the story of the covenant between God and his chosen people. Yet he also knew the more recent history of ten Israelite tribes being dispersed by the Assyrians. Suddenly he was ordered to prophesy that the two surviving tribes in Judah would undergo a similar trial. In Jeremiah's own lifetime, Babylonian armies would desecrate the holy city of Jerusalem and take captive many more Israelites.

Has God abandoned the covenant? Has he cast aside his chosen people? In this chapter, Jeremiah receives a dream sequence that hints at an answer. He saw that a "remnant" would survive the Babylonian invasion. God had not permanently rejected his people, but was allowing them to go through temporary punishment for the sake of purging. Moreover, God promised that the future of the Israelites would be far grander than anything in the past.

Bible interpreters disagree on the full meaning of these promises. Some things are clear: For example, God promised a "new covenant" to replace and improve on the old, broken one. Hebrews 8 quotes a key passage from this chapter in Jeremiah and applies the prophecy to Jesus, who made possible the *new* covenant and its grand forgiveness.

But what of the predictions that seem to apply, geographically, to the land of Palestine? Some of the exiled Israelites, led by Ezra and Nehemiah, did eventually return from captivity in Babylon, but that sparse resettlement of a devastated land hardly calls to mind the glorious new society described here. Jewish scholars disagree on the meaning: some point to the modern-day state of Israel as a direct fulfillment of this prophecy, while others violently disagree. And some Christian theologians believe that these promises, under the new covenant, apply to the Church in a more general sense, and not to the Jewish race and its settlement of the land.

Jeremiah did not get a detailed blueprint of future history, but he did get a resounding confirmation of how God feels about his people.

LIFE QUESTION: *Does God have a "covenant" with us today? What does it promise?*

Prophet's Perils

Jeremiah had good reason for being a weeping, balky prophet. Four kings succeeded Josiah, and each of them gave the prophet a hard time. One king scheduled a private reading of Jeremiah's prophecies in his winter apartment. As each scroll was read, the king casually hacked it to pieces with a knife and tossed it into the fireplace (36:23). On other occasions the prophet himself was beaten and put in stocks, or locked in a dungeon, or, as this chapter relates, thrown in a well. The best state Jeremiah could hope for was house arrest or confinement in the king's courtyard.

The mistreatment only served to harden Jeremiah's resolve. He would curse his tormentors even as they released him from the stocks. Evidently, he reserved his fears and doubts for God's ears alone.

The events in this chapter took place in Jerusalem, in the midst of a terrible two-year siege by the Babylonians. The city's starving residents, barely clinging to survival, had resorted to cannibalism. City officials were frantically trying to improve morale and whip up courage. Little wonder they objected to Jeremiah's dour advice: "We're going to lose anyway—might as well defect over the walls, or open the gates and let the Babylonians in."

The following chapter (39) tells of Jeremiah's prophecies coming true. Babylon's army did breach the walls, and then captured and tortured the weak King Zedekiah. The conquerors treated Jeremiah with respect, however, having heard of his counsel to surrender.

Not long after the fall of Jerusalem, a gang of Israelites rebelled against their captors and ran to Egypt, with the angry prophet in tow. They thought they had reached safety. But in his last recorded words, Jeremiah, a browbeaten seventy-year-old, announced that those refugees would meet a tragic end. They ignored him—just like everyone else in Jeremiah's hapless career.

LIFE QUESTION: *What do you think Jeremiah would have said about the "prosperity theology" some Christians preach today?*

Debating God

*E*veryone has a built-in sense of justice. If a careless driver runs down a small child and nonchalantly drives on, other drivers will follow in hot pursuit. *He can't get away with that!* We may disagree on specific rules of fairness, but we all follow some inner code.

And, frankly, often life seems unfair. What child "deserves" to grow up in the slums of Calcutta, or Rio de Janeiro, or the East Bronx? Why should people like Adolf Hitler, Joseph Stalin, and Saddam Hussein get away with tyrannizing millions of people? Why are some kind, gentle people struck down in the prime of life while other meaner people live into cantankerous old age?

We all ask different versions of such questions. The prophet named Habakkuk asked them of God directly, and got a no-holds-barred reply. Habakkuk did not mince words. He demanded that God explain why he wasn't responding to the injustice, violence, and evil that the prophet could see all around him.

God answered with the same message he had told Jeremiah, that he would send the Babylonians to punish Judah. But such words hardly reassured Habakkuk, for the Babylonians were ruthless, savage people. Could this be justice—using an even more evil nation to punish Judah?

The book of Habakkuk does not solve the problem of evil. But Habakkuk's conversations with God convinced him of one certainty: God had not lost control. As a God of justice, he could not let evil win. First, he would deal with the Babylonians. Then, later, he would intervene with great force, shaking the very foundations of the earth until no sign of injustice remained.

In the course of his "debate" with God, Habakkuk learned new lessons about faith, which are beautifully expressed in the last chapter. God's answers so satisfied Habakkuk that his book, which begins with a complaint, ends with one of the most beautiful songs in the Bible.

LIFE QUESTION: *What do you find most troubling about God's answer to Habakkuk? Most satisfying? Do you have similar questions?*

In Shock

I am the man who has seen affliction . . ." this chapter begins, and that doleful sentence captures this entire book. Judah's king is now shackled and blinded, his princes slaughtered. Jerusalem—the capital city, the holy city—is no more. The poet writes this book in a state of dazed grief. He wanders the empty streets, piled high with corpses, and tries to make sense of a tragedy that defies all comprehension.

But beyond the human tragedy, a different kind of distress gnawed at the author. Babylonian soldiers had entered the temple—pagans in the Most Holy Place!—looted it, then burned it to the ground. The dream of the covenant died on that day. Historians record that as the Babylonians entered the temple they swept the empty air with their spears, seeking the unseen Jewish God. But they found nothing. God had given up; he had fled the premises. Jews still mourn the event: Each year on the anniversary of the day the temple was destroyed, the Orthodox read the book of Lamentations aloud.

The tone of this anonymous book may sound familiar, for the prophet Jeremiah is the likely author. He is an old man, with shriveled skin and broken bones. He has been hunted, jailed, tortured, thrown in a pit and left for dead. Yet nothing can match the grief he feels now as he stares, not at his own wounds, but at the gaping wounds of Jerusalem.

God is an enemy, the prophet concludes, in an outburst familiar to any reader of Jeremiah. He lets his venom spill out. And yet, in the middle of this dark chapter, the author remembers what he once learned about God in brighter, happier times. He recalls the goodness of God, the love, the compassion. In the midst of this bleak book come words that a writer later crafted into a hymn: "Great is Thy Faithfulness." At the moment of terrible tragedy, those qualities of God may seem very far away—but where else can we turn? As Lamentations shows, without God's hope, there is no hope.

LIFE QUESTION: *In your darkest times, do your thoughts turn to God? What helps you find relief?*

No Room to Gloat

Remember, O LORD, what the Edomites did on the day Jerusalem fell. 'Tear it down,' they cried, 'tear it down to its foundations!'" (Psalm 137:7). Survivors of the sacking of Jerusalem would never forget the reactions of their neighbors the Edomites, who had watched the carnage with open glee. The Edomites cheered the conquering Babylonian army, looted the fleeing refugees, and helped plunder Jerusalem. Psalm 137, one of the saddest passages in the Bible, voices the Israelites' acrid bitterness over this offense.

To rub salt in Judah's wounds, the Edomites were actually distant relatives. Their nation traced back to the feud between twin brothers Jacob and Esau. While Jacob fathered the Israelites, Esau, having traded away his birthright for a meal, moved to desolate mountain country and founded the nation of Edom. The twins' descendants continued the quarrel for hundreds of years, and now the Edomites were gloating over the Israelites' calamity. True children of Esau, they thought primarily of the immediate gain available to them from plunder.

The Edomites' attitude contrasts sharply with the sorrow expressed in the book of Lamentations. And Obadiah, the shortest book in the Old Testament, makes clear that the Edomites would pay for their callousness and cruelty: "As you have done, it will be done to you." Those who had betrayed Judah would be repaid with treachery from their own allies.

Obadiah predicted opposite futures for Israel and Edom. According to him, downtrodden Israel would rise again, but Edom would disappear from the face of the earth. History bore out the latter prediction in 70 A.D., when Roman legions destroyed the last remnant of Edomites during a siege of Jerusalem.

LIFE QUESTION: *Edom was basing its security on its location "in the clefts of the rocks." What do people around you base their security on?*

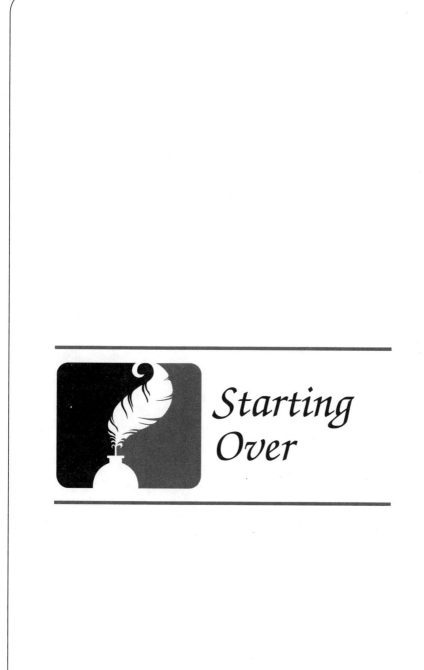

Starting Over

Prophet in Exile

KEY VERSE: *Like the appearance of a rainbow in the clouds on a rainy day, so was the radiance around him. This was the appearance of the likeness of the glory of the LORD. (Ezek. 1:28)*

About the same time that Jeremiah, Habakkuk, and Obadiah were prophesying in Judah, a man named Ezekiel received a dramatic call to minister to their unfortunate countrymen in exile. The Babylonian army had been pillaging Judah for twenty years before the fall of Jerusalem, and Ezekiel was among the first wave of captives taken to Babylon, nearly 500 miles away. He lived with the Israelites in a refugee settlement beside a river.

Like refugees everywhere, those in Babylon longed for nothing more than a chance to return to their homeland. They received letters of advice and comfort from the prophet Jeremiah. They cringed at reports of rebellion by Judah's kings, fearful that any rebellion might arouse the wrath of Babylon. They wondered anxiously whether their beleaguered nation could survive.

An uprooted, dispirited people such as these needed a strong, authoritative voice, and in Ezekiel they got exactly that. As a young man in training for the priesthood, he had found his career plans interrupted by the foreign deportations. What good was a priest in Babylon when the temple was in Jerusalem? God summoned Ezekiel to a new role, as prophet to the Jews in exile.

Ezekiel begins with a description so unearthly that some have suggested the prophet saw a UFO. Indeed, there are some similarities: glowing lights, quick movements, inhuman figures. But, there are differences, too, in this account of a "close encounter." This majestic being was not mysteriously rushing off to disappear. He wanted to be known by everyone. And he had chosen the prophet Ezekiel as the one privileged to make him known.

Confronted with such splendor, Ezekiel fell on his face. But the Spirit of God raised him to his feet and gave him an assignment. After that vision, Ezekiel would never again wonder about a question that often bothered the other refugees: Had God abandoned them? Ezekiel's encounter of the closest kind convinced him permanently that God still cared about his people—even the exiles in Babylon.

LIFE QUESTION: *Have you ever felt "abandoned" by God? What helped you feel less so?*

107

Toughening Up

KEY VERSE:

Do not be afraid, though briers and thorns are all around you and you live among scorpions. Do not be afraid of what they say or terrified by them, though they are a rebellious house. (Ezek. 2:6)

Orthodox Jewish rabbis forbid anyone under the age of thirty to read the first three chapters of Ezekiel. No young person, they reason, is ready for such a direct encounter with the glory of the Lord. Indeed, Ezekiel himself barely survived the experience. He kept falling on his face, and was knocked speechless for seven days.

Such exalted revelations were part of God's training regimen, a process of toughening up the prophet for a demanding task. With Isaiah sawn in two and Jeremiah thrown in a well, the prophets of Judah had plenty of reason for alarm. What might befall Ezekiel as he took the word of God to an ornery people in the heart of enemy territory? To embolden him, God gave Ezekiel an experience he would never forget or doubt, no matter what difficulties he might confront.

God warned Ezekiel that few Israelites, if any, would listen to his message. He had to become as stubborn and unyielding as the audience he addressed. As a result, Ezekiel lived a lonely life. People thought of him as a dreamy storyteller, and scoffed at his pessimistic predictions of Jerusalem's fall. Still, despite the negative tone of his prophecies, Ezekiel never once lost hope. He could see past the tragedies of the present day to a future time when God would restore his people and his temple.

Ezekiel's faith could not be shaken, because he had received a vision of the glory of the Lord. Due to his priestly training, he undoubtedly recognized the light, the fire, and the glow—Israelites had seen those images in the pillar of fire in the wilderness, and in the cloud that descended into Solomon's temple. Now the nation was in shambles, its chief citizens in exile. But even there, in Babylon, the glory of the Lord appeared to Ezekiel. That experience alone gave him the courage he would need to fight off the enemies that surrounded him.

LIFE QUESTION: *What obstacles do people face today when they try to deliver a message from God?*

Draw Large and Shout

When someone asked Flannery O'Connor why she filled her novels with such exaggerated, eccentric characters she replied, "To the hard of hearing you shout, and for the almost-blind you draw large and startling figures." The same answer may help explain the oddities of Ezekiel. He, too, faced a dense audience who had little tolerance for his message. And God instructed him to use some bizarre methods to get that message across.

The book records twelve public "object lessons" acted out by the prophet. For example, one year he lay on his side every day, bound by ropes and facing a clay model of Jerusalem. Strange? When a car is headed toward the edge of a cliff, you may scream and gesture so wildly that people think you insane. So it was with Ezekiel, who would do anything to force people to pay attention.

The first part of Ezekiel mainly concerns the political situation back in the homeland of Judah. False prophets were assuring the exiles that God would never allow his temple or holy city to be destroyed. Ezekiel blasted these phony optimists and broadcasted God's plan of judgment in strong words and public protests. He took no great delight in the doomsday message. Twice, seeing the future, he fell down, crying out in horror (9:8; 11:13). In this chapter, when God tells him to cook food on human excrement as a symbolic act, he is too shocked to agree.

Ezekiel delivered an undiluted message from God, presenting it in a way that the Israelites could not ignore. Ezekiel's exaggerated style says much about the One who gave him orders. God would not let go of his people until he had done all in his power to turn them around. No device was too undignified, no carnival ploy too corny, as long as he had the slightest hope of breaking through. "As surely as I live, declares the Sovereign LORD, I take no pleasure in the death of the wicked, but rather that they turn from their ways and live. Turn! Turn from your evil ways! Why will you die, O house of Israel?" (33:11).

LIFE QUESTION: *How does God get your attention?*

Dry Bones

*W*hy would Jerusalem be destroyed? Why would all Judah's enemies come to a violent end? So that they would "know that I am the LORD." This is the phrase echoed over sixty times in the book of Ezekiel. In a sudden change of tone, God used that same phrase to explain why he would bring about a time of future happiness.

After all the gloom, Ezekiel at last got to pronounce words of great joy and hope. In the early days, he alone had prophesied doom, and no one had listened. Then, for a period of seven years he maintained a virtual silence. But now he opened his mouth again, and bright words of hope issued forth.

Ezekiel experienced a sudden surge in popularity among the exiles, since he alone had predicted current events accurately. As people flocked to hear his words, he scolded them for their unchanged hearts, then confirmed the rumor of good news to come.

No part of Ezekiel captures that message of hope more effectively than this startling vision of the valley of dry bones. Like a graveyard of scattered, bleached bones coming gloriously to life, the deadest of the dead will live.

Ezekiel's original audience was still trying to absorb the staggering news that the temple had been razed, with God apparently departed. But Ezekiel assured them God had not given up; the split kingdoms of Judah and Israel would join together again at last. God was coming back to his home, to live with his people.

The book ends with a shining vision of a new Jerusalem arising from the ruins of the old. Scholars disagree on whether Ezekiel's words apply literally, or symbolically, to the nation of Israel. But it is clear that the good news will affect the whole world. The triumphant name of that new city says it all: "And the name of the city from that time on will be: THE LORD IS THERE."

LIFE QUESTION: *Where are you spiritually? With the dry bones? Barely stirring? Alive and well?*

Enemy Employers

Whereas Ezekiel spent his days preaching (and acting out) sermons to the Jewish exiles, Daniel was recruited for a job in the king's palace.

In fact, Daniel's life in the palace more closely resembles that of the ancient character Joseph, who also rose to a position of prominence in a foreign government. As this chapter underscores, Daniel achieved success without bending his own principles of integrity. Somehow he managed to thrive in an environment marked by ambition and intrigue, while still holding to his high-minded Jewish ideals.

The Babylonians did their best to purge the young Jews of their heritage. They forced on them new, pagan names, and plied them with wine and food that had been offered to idols. Even the study course for diplomats-in-training was distasteful to a Jew: It covered sorcery, magic, and a pagan, multigod religion. Daniel and his three friends overcame these obstacles and excelled enough to attract the attention of the king, who had to take notice: The four were ten times more impressive than anyone else in the kingdom.

Taken together, the biblical prophets offer not one, but many models of how a person can serve both God and the state. On the one extreme stand men like Amos and Elijah, who, as outsiders, railed against the evils of society. Others, such as Jeremiah and Nathan, gave occasional counsel to kings, but kept a safe distance. Isaiah and Samuel, however, became official advisers of kings. And in this book the prophet Daniel shows that a person can keep pure even while working within a tyrannical regime.

For at least sixty-six years, Daniel served pagan kings with great diligence and resourcefulness. Yet he never once compromised his faith, even when threatened with death. The Bible offers no better model of how to live among people who do not share or respect your beliefs.

LIFE QUESTION: *When have you taken a difficult or unpopular stand as a matter of integrity?*

Well-timed Rescue

Stories from Daniel have become famous, and in fact any of the first six chapters would make a script for a thriller. In this story Daniel's three friends saw king Nebuchadnezzar's decree as a bottom-line issue of spiritual integrity that brought their dual loyalties into irreconcilable conflict. In this instance, they could not serve both the kingdom of God and the kingdom of Babylon. There could be no compromise.

Idolatry was, in fact, the stubborn sin of Judah that had brought on the Babylonian punishment in the first place. The Jews could never expect God's blessing if they chose to bow down to Nebuchadnezzar and his gold image. The uncompromising response of Daniel's friends shows that the Babylonian captivity was having a "refiner's fire" effect on a whole generation of Jewish exiles.

The book of Daniel makes for exciting reading because, at this most precarious time in Israelite history, God let loose with a burst of miraculous activity: supernatural dreams, handwriting on the wall, rescues from a fiery furnace and a lions' den. Not since Elisha's day had the Israelites seen such signs and wonders.

The story of the fiery furnace has a happy ending, far beyond anything the three courageous Jews might have hoped for. Not only did they survive; the event ensured that Nebuchadnezzar would treat the Jewish religion with tolerance throughout his reign.

The Israelites were still thinking of God in terms of their own small community, but God had never intended for his blessings to stop with the Jews. When he had first revealed the covenant to Abraham, he had promised that Abraham's offspring would bless the whole earth (Genesis 12:3). Ironically, at a time of deep humiliation, while living as unwilling captives in Babylon, the Jews began to convince others that their God deserved honor. The proclamations by Nebuchadnezzar and later Darius (6:26–27) honored God more than anything a king of Judah had done in years.

LIFE QUESTION: *What do you learn about faith from the reply of Daniel's friends (vv. 15–18)?*

Like Father, Like Son

KEY VERSE: *"This is what these words mean: Mene: God has numbered the days of your reign and brought it to an end. Tekel: You have been weighed on the scales and found wanting. Peres: Your kingdom is divided and given to the Medes and Persians." (Dan. 5:26–28)*

A miracle may make someone sit up and take notice, but it surely does not guarantee long-term change. Despite Nebuchadnezzar's new-found enthusiasm for the God of the Hebrews, in time he apparently forgot all about his religious zeal.

The king's son Belshazzar, who had grown up in the midst of the flurry of miracles, had an even shorter memory. Chapter 5 introduces the new king at a state orgy as he boozes it up with a thousand nobles and assorted women. They were carousing in a kind of "hurricane party" to show their disdain over reports of enemy armies advancing on the capital. The party even included a religious element, after a fashion: They worshiped idols, and used sacred relics stolen from the temple in Jerusalem to hold their wine.

Belshazzar's raucous party provided the setting for a scene straight out of a horror film: human fingers, eerily disconnected from any hand, wrote a message on the wall. The king trembled and turned pale, but it took the queen to remember the supernatural gifts of an old Jewish prophet. Daniel hadn't changed a bit over the years. He respectfully declined the king's bribes, but interpreted the dream anyway, after delivering an impromptu sermon.

That night, Daniel got another high-ranking appointment to the government of a tyrant. But the job didn't last long. The same night, Babylon fell victim to a sneak attack, and Darius the Mede took over the kingdom.

A phrase has come down from this story—"That's the handwriting on the wall"—to signify a final warning just before the end. The prophets of Israel and Judah had tried to interpret God's "handwriting" for their countrymen, with little success, and God had used Babylon to punish them. Now Babylon, having ignored the warnings of a spiritual giant like Daniel, was itself due for punishment. They had ignored handwriting on the wall long enough.

LIFE QUESTION: *What "handwriting on the wall" might our society be ignoring?*

The Lions' Den

KEY VERSE: "My God sent his angel, and he shut the mouths of the lions. They have not hurt me, because I was found innocent in his sight. Nor have I ever done any wrong before you, O king." (Dan. 6:22)

After six decades of service, Daniel finally faced a situation like the one his three friends in the fiery furnace had faced—an unresolvable conflict between the law of God and the law of the land. During those years Daniel had lost much of his Jewish heritage and had even taken on a Babylonian name. Yet, although he could hardly worship God in the way he wished, at the temple in Jerusalem, his devotion to God never wavered. In defiance of the king's new law, the old prophet kept on pointing himself toward Jerusalem three times a day in prayer.

The story of Daniel in the lions' den has special meaning for Jews and Christians because, sadly, history has repeated itself so often. The Roman Empire, Stalin's Russia, Hitler's Germany, China—they've all taken their turn at restricting worship, yet the church has survived, and even thrived, during times of intense persecution. Not everyone who undergoes religious persecution receives miraculous deliverance like Daniel's. But, all together, the martyrs have given a witness to the watching world that true faith cannot be stamped out, no matter what the penalty.

A miracle spared Daniel's life; an even greater miracle took place in those around him. Stirred by Daniel's faith, the Persian ruler issued a decree that everyone in his kingdom must fear and reverence "the God of Daniel." Soon, the same empire that had passed laws against Jewish worship would escort the Jewish exiles back to their homeland and allow them to rebuild the temple.

The harsh times in Babylon had their effect on the Jewish community as well. Led by the examples of people such as Daniel, they began a new practice of meeting together in "synagogues" to study the Law and to pray. And they would return to Palestine purged of the sin that had brought them so much anguish: Jews never again were known to practice idolatry. The refining fire had done its work.

LIFE QUESTION: *Do you know of any irreconcilable conflicts between the law of the land and the law of God today?*

Back in Jerusalem

While some people, like Daniel, prospered in exile, no true Israelite ever felt totally at peace there. Always, a longing gnawed inside, a longing for home, and for the temple of God. As one poet in exile wrote, "If I forget you, O Jerusalem, may my right hand forget its skill. May my tongue cling to the roof of my mouth if I do not remember you, if I do not consider Jerusalem my highest joy" (Psalm 137:5).

Daniel's new boss, in keeping with the Persian policy of religious tolerance, granted permission for the first wave of Jewish exiles to return to Jerusalem, and the book of Ezra tells their story. And yet the sight that greeted the returning exiles in Jerusalem made them very sad: The city was a ghost town, burned and pillaged years before by the conquering Babylonians. The temple of God was a mound of rubble.

The settlers went to work at once, setting temple reconstruction as their highest priority. They had hope: The Persians had even given back the pilfered silver and gold temple articles. When the Jews finally laid the foundation, the sound of their shouting could be heard from far away. The temple, after all, was the place where they would meet God and, as such, symbolized a new start with him.

Yet the shouts of joy mingled with loud cries of weeping as well. The older returnees, those who remembered Solomon's temple in all its splendor, wept at the comparison. They had lost political independence, and needed permission from a foreign government just to rebuild the temple. The Jews had regained only a tiny portion of their former territory. They were very far from the glory days of David and Solomon.

The book of Ezra thus introduces a new period in the Israelites' history—a period in which they became more like a "church" than a nation. Their leaders focused energy not on fighting enemy armies, but on fighting sin and spiritual compromise. They feared repeating the mistakes that had sent them into exile.

LIFE QUESTION: *If a modern city burned to the ground, what buildings would likely be replaced first?*

A Needed Boost

The burst of energy described in Ezra did not last long. Opposition soon arose among the tribes bordering Israel, who did not look kindly on the resurgence of a traditional enemy. The temple project especially alarmed them, in view of all the stories they had heard about the miraculous power of Israel's God. And surely, they reasoned, a rebuilt temple would only inflame the Israelites' religious zeal. Even Israel's protector, Persia, began to waver on its promises to the Jews.

In the face of this stiff opposition, the Jews lost enthusiasm, or rather redirected their enthusiasm toward other projects. Just a few years after the exiles' return, work on the temple ground to a halt. The Jews began to concentrate instead on building their own homes and regaining their former prosperity. They had forgotten the original motive for returning to Jerusalem.

About twenty years after the first migration, a prophet named Haggai appeared in Jerusalem to confront the growing apathy and confusion. He did not rage like Jeremiah or act out public object lessons like Ezekiel. He simply urged these pioneers to give careful thought to their situation.

Haggai put things simply and logically. The settlers had worked hard, but what had it earned them? Their crops were unsuccessful. Their money disappeared as soon as they earned it. Haggai's diagnosis: mistaken priorities. The Israelites needed to put God first, and for starters that meant rebuilding his temple. God's reputation was at stake. If the temple symbolized God's presence, how could he be properly honored when his house lay in ruins?

Amazingly, Haggai struck an immediate chord of response in his audience. Prophets before him, such as Amos, Isaiah, or Jeremiah, had spoken for decades without seeing such a heartfelt reaction.

LIFE QUESTION: *What tends to distract us from spiritual priorities?*

Raising Sights

KEY VERSE: *"Then Jerusalem will be called the City of Truth, and the mountain of the LORD Almighty will be called the Holy Mountain." (Zech. 8:3)*

*A*nother, younger prophet named Zechariah joined Haggai in his campaign to lift the spirits of the settlers in Jerusalem (Ezra 5:1 lists both these prophets by name). The two had a similar message, but a different approach. Whereas Haggai asked the Jews to look around at their current conditions and then make some needed changes, Zechariah called them to look beyond the present and envision a new Jerusalem, a "City of Truth."

At the time, the pioneers were focusing on immediate goals: the next planting of crops, basic shelter for their families, repopulating the deserted city. Zechariah lifted their sights toward a far more glorious future, when Jerusalem would be a light to the world and people from many nations would stream to the city "because we have heard that God is with you." The prophet gives his prescription for reaching such a state: The new society must be built on justice, honesty, integrity, and peace.

It took years to rebuild the city of Jerusalem, and centuries for Israel to regain some form of political independence. The Jews who labored so hard must have asked themselves often, "Is this all God has in mind for us?" Zechariah replied with a resounding "No!" He insisted that the small refugee community in fact held the key to the world's future: Their new beginning would lead the way to a Messiah who would bring hope to the whole earth.

Following Haggai's lead, Zechariah seized upon the need to rebuild the temple as a vital first step. These prophets saw that as long as the temple lay in ruins, Israel's distinctive character as a people of God was suspect. Together, the two men had a remarkable effect on their countrymen. At their urging, the Jews organized to build again, and within four years the temple was complete. Once more the nation had a central reminder of its original covenant with God.

LIFE QUESTION: *How well does your community measure up to the society God describes in this chapter?*

A Man for All Seasons

KEY VERSE: *"Come, let us rebuild the wall of Jerusalem, and we will no longer be in disgrace." (Neh. 2:17)*

Sixty-five years passed. The Jews had a temple in Jerusalem, yes, but very little beyond that. The holy city was sparsely occupied; most Jews had settled in the outlying villages and towns rather than inside its crumbling walls. Indeed, with all the intermarriage and mixing with foreigners, the entire community seemed on the verge of losing its unique identity. The Jews' cultural and religious heritage was slipping away.

What could stop the downhill slide? One man, a Jewish exile who had stayed behind in Babylon, had an idea. Like Daniel before him, Nehemiah had risen in the ranks of a foreign government (Persia), and was prospering. Nevertheless, his heart was with his countrymen back in Jerusalem, and when he heard the dismaying reports from that city he felt compelled to act. He obtained the king's permission to lead an expedition to Jerusalem with the goal of rebuilding the city's wall.

In an age when nomadic warriors posed a constant danger, a wall offered a city its only security. It was for lack of a wall that the Jews had scattered among neighbors and were now facing permanent assimilation into other cultures. By constructing a wall, Nehemiah could help make Jerusalem into a sacred city again and protect its residents by controlling who else came and went.

Strictly speaking, Nehemiah was not a prophet, although he was surely a man of God. He did not act without prayer, and he did not pray without acting. Although he had enormous skills in management and leadership, he did not seek after earthly status—if he had, he never would have left Persia.

Nehemiah improvised as he went, meeting each new challenge with a combination of business savvy, courage, and dependence on God. He mobilized work crews, fought off opposition, reformed the court system, purified religious practices, and, when necessary, rallied the troops with stirring speeches. And he did all this while "on leave" from his responsibilities as statesman in the Persian court.

LIFE QUESTION: *Do you see any secrets of success in this record of Nehemiah's actions?*

Mourning into Joy

Nehemiah alone was an impressive leader, but when paired with Ezra he was downright indomitable. The two made a perfect combination. Nehemiah, emboldened by good political connections, inspired others with his hands-on management style and his fearless optimism. Ezra relied more on moral force than on personality. He could trace his priestly lineage all the way back to Moses' brother Aaron, and seemed singularly determined to restore integrity to that office.

The action in this chapter takes place after Nehemiah has completed the arduous task of repairing the wall. The Jews, safe at last from their enemies, gather together in hopes of regaining some sense of national identity. As spiritual leader, Ezra is chosen to address the huge crowd. He stands on a newly built platform and begins to read from a document nearly 1000 years old, the scroll that contains the Israelites' original covenant with God.

As Ezra reads the ancient words, a sound of weeping begins to rise, spreading through the multitude. The Bible does not explain the reason for the tears. Were the people feeling guilt over their long history of breaking that covenant? Or nostalgia over the favored days when Israel had full independence? Whatever the reason, this was no time for tears. Nehemiah and Ezra sent out orders to prepare for a huge feast and celebration. God wanted joy, not mourning. His chosen people were being rebuilt, just as surely as the stone walls of Jerusalem had been rebuilt.

The central image of this chapter—a lone figure atop a wooden platform reading from a scroll—came to symbolize the Jewish race. They were becoming "people of the Book." The Jews had not regained the territory and splendor their nation once enjoyed under David and Solomon. The temple they had painstakingly constructed would eventually fall to looters, just like the one it replaced. But they would never forget the lesson of Ezra. He became the prototype for a new leader of the Jews: the scribe, a student of Scripture.

LIFE QUESTION: *How important is the Bible in your own life?*

Jews Who Stayed Behind

Not every Jewish exile took the opportunity to return to the homeland. Some had put down roots during the half-century of Babylonian Captivity, and when the more tolerant Persian regime took over, many of these decided to stay. (Communities of Jews in present-day Iraq and Syria still trace their ancestry to this group of exiles.) This adventure story concerns one such Jew who stayed behind, a beautiful woman named Esther.

The Jews in Persia faced a grave crisis. Their success had attracted so much jealousy that a powerful man was leading a conspiracy to kill every Jew in the land.

Although the book of Esther never once mentions the word *God,* the story highlights the many "coincidences" that worked together on the Jews' behalf. By the "accident" of her beauty and the "accident" of the former queen's dismissal, Esther had risen from obscurity to become queen of the Persian Empire. She alone, of all the Jews, had access to the king.

Yet in those days, a queen did not easily stand up to her husband—especially a husband like Xerxes, who had already summarily dismissed one queen for insubordination. By intervening for the sake of her race, Esther might be putting her own life in jeopardy. This portion of the book spells out Esther's dilemma, and tells the decision she finally reached. The rest of the book records a series of twists of plot: The Jews are spared, even honored, and the original conspirator is hanged in their place.

Esther's story is a thrilling chapter in the story of God's love for the Jews. While no other group has been so persecuted, no other group has shown the Jews' ability to overcome adversity. How? Esther reveals God's exquisite timing, combined with the courage of individuals who "happened" to be in the right place at the right time.

LIFE QUESTION: *Someone has called coincidences "God's way of working anonymously." Do you tend to give God credit for the "coincidences" in your life?*

Crushed Hopes

*M*alachi is the last Old Testament voice, and his book serves as a good prelude to the next 400 years of biblical silence. From the Israelites' point of view, those four centuries could be termed "the era of lowered expectations." They had returned to the land, but that land remained a backwater province under the domination of several imperial armies. The grand future of triumph and world peace described by the prophets seemed a distant pipe dream. Even the restored temple caused stabs of nostalgic pain: It hardly rivaled Solomon's majestic building, and no one had seen God's glory descend on this new temple as it had in Solomon's day.

A general malaise set in among the Jews, a low-grade disappointment with God that showed in their complaints and actions. They were not "big" sinners like the people before the Exile, who had practiced child sacrifice and brought idols into the temple. They went through the motions of their religion, but had lost contact with the God whom the religion was all about.

Malachi is written in the form of a dialogue, with the "children" of Israel bringing their grievances to God, the Father. They were questioning God's love and his fairness. One gripe bothered them more than any: Following God had not brought the anticipated reward.

In reply, Malachi calls his people to rise above their selfishness and to trust the God of the covenant; he has not abandoned his treasured possession. "Test me," says God, "and see if I will not throw open the floodgates of heaven and pour out so much blessing that you will not have room enough for it."

At least some of Malachi's message took hold. During the next 400 years, reform movements like the Pharisees became increasingly devoted to keeping the Law. Unfortunately, many of them would cling fiercely to that Law even when Jesus, the "messenger of the covenant" prophesied by Malachi, brought a new message of forgiveness and grace.

LIFE QUESTION: *What treatments does God offer for the Israelites' "lukewarm" faith?*

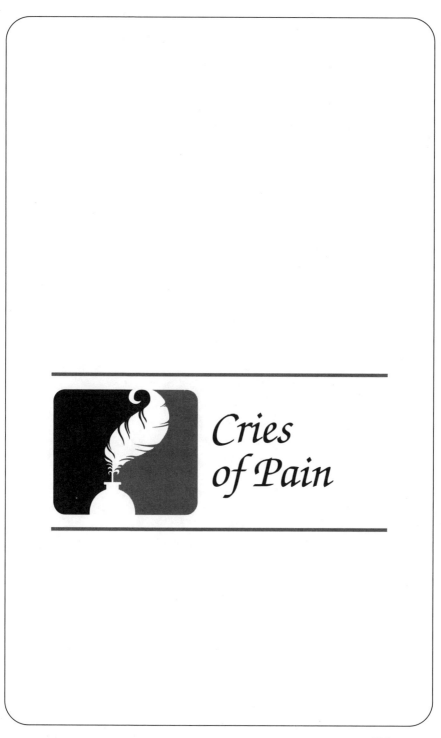

Cries
of Pain

Is God Unfair?

KEY VERSE:

Does Job fear God for nothing? . . . . Have you not put a hedge around him and his household and everything he has? . . . But stretch out your hand and strike everything he has, and he will surely curse you to your face. (Job 1:9–11)

One book of the Bible is virtually ageless. It relates the story of Job, a rich "patriarch" who could have lived in Abraham's time, but whose story was probably reduced to this poetic form hundreds of years later, during Israel's literary Golden Age. Regardless, the book raises questions so urgent and universal that it speaks to every era.

Job's story centers around a question that haunted the Jews from the earliest days, when they were first chosen as God's covenant people. Somehow, they expected better treatment. Job had the courage to voice the question aloud—*Is God unfair?*—and no one has asked that question more eloquently or profoundly.

The book seems meant to explore the outer limits of unfairness. Job, the most upright, outstanding man in all the earth, must endure the worst calamities. He suffers unbearable punishment—but for what? What has he done wrong?

The book reads like a detective story in which the readers know far more than the central characters. The very first chapter answers Job's main concern: He has done nothing to deserve such suffering. We, the readers, know that, but nobody tells Job and his friends. As the prologue reveals, Job was involved in a cosmic test, a contest proposed in heaven but staged on earth.

Satan had claimed that people love God *only* because of his good gifts. According to Satan, no one would ever follow God apart from some selfish gain. *Of course,* Job was blameless and upright; he was also rich and healthy. Remove those good things from Job's life, Satan challenged, and watch Job's faith melt away.

God's reputation is on the line in this book; it rests suspensefully on the response of a devastated, miserable man. Will Job continue to trust God, even as his world crashes down around him? Will he believe in a God of justice, even when life seems grotesquely unfair?

LIFE QUESTION: *When have you questioned "why bad things happen to good people"?*

Blast from the Storm

*L*ike all grieving persons, Job drifted on emotional currents, alternately whining, exploding, cajoling, and collapsing into self-pity. Sometimes he agreed with his friends, who blamed Job himself for his suffering, and sometimes he violently disagreed. Occasionally, in the midst of deepest despair, he would come up with a statement of brilliant hope.

Nearly every argument on the problem of pain appears somewhere in the book of Job, but the arguing never seemed to help Job much. His was a crisis of relationship more than a crisis of intellectual doubt. *Could he trust God?* Job wanted one thing above all else: an appearance by the one Person who could explain his miserable fate. He wanted to meet God himself, face to face.

Eventually, as this chapter relates, Job got his wish. God showed up in person. He timed his entrance with perfect irony, just as Elihu was expounding on why Job had no right to expect a visit from God.

No one—not Job, nor any of his friends—was prepared for what God had to say. Job had saved up a long list of questions, but it was God, not Job, who asked the questions. Brushing aside thirty-five chapters' worth of debates on the problem of pain, God plunged instead into a majestic poem on the wonders of the natural world. He guided Job through the gallery of creation, pointing out with pride such favorites as mountain goats, wild donkeys, ostriches, and eagles.

Above all, God's speech defined the vast difference between a God of all creation and one puny man like Job. "Do you have an arm like God's?" he asked at one point (40:9). God reeled off natural phenomena—the solar system, constellations, thunderstorms, wild animals—that Job could not begin to explain. God's point was obvious: If you can't comprehend the visible world you live in, how dare you expect to comprehend a world you cannot even see!

LIFE QUESTION: *Does God's reply to Job surprise you? In Job's place, what kind of answer would you have wanted from God?*

Job's Happy Ending

Then Job replied to the LORD: "I know that you can do all things; no plan of yours can be thwarted." (Job 42:1–2)

What God said in his speech to Job was not nearly so important as the mere fact that he showed up. His presence spectacularly answered Job's biggest question: Is anybody out there? "Surely I spoke of things I did not understand," Job confessed, "things too wonderful for me to know." Catching sight of the big picture at last, Job repented in dust and ashes.

God had some words of correction for Job: No one, not Job and especially not his friends, had the evidence needed to make judgments about how he ran the world. But mainly God praised Job, calling him "my servant."

Satan had wagered with God that Job would "surely curse you to your face." He lost. Despite all that happened, Job did not curse God. He clung to his belief in a just God even though everything in his experience contradicted it. Significantly, Job spoke his contrite words *before* any of his losses had been restored, while still sitting in a pile of ashes, naked, covered with sores. He had learned to believe even in the dark, with no hope of reward.

The book of Job ends with some surprising twists. Job's friends, who had spouted all the right pieties and cliches, had to plead for forgiveness. Job, who had raged and cried out, received twice as much as he ever had before: 14,000 sheep, 6000 camels, 1000 donkeys, and 10 new children.

The book of Job gave much comfort to Jews during the harsh period between the Old and New Testaments. It demonstrated the important lesson that not all suffering comes as punishment; a person's trials may, in fact, be used to win a great spiritual victory. And the happy ending of Job also echoed the promises of the prophets, awakening hopes for a future time of peace and restoration.

Christians, looking back, see yet another message in Job, who stands as an early prototype of the Messiah. Job, the best man of his day, suffered terribly; Jesus, a perfect man, would suffer even more.

LIFE QUESTION: *Have you experienced any Job-like trials in your life? What was their result?*

Who's in Charge?

The book of Job concerns the sufferings of one man. The prophets of Israel and Judah spoke to the sufferings of an entire race. Most of the Jews were scattered across the Middle East, dispersed by Assyrian and Babylonian armies. The minority who had returned to Jerusalem lived under the total domination of a foreign government in Persia. The same questions Job had asked while scratching himself with shards of pottery, the Jews asked about their race. Had God abandoned them? Would they have a future?

The Jews' hope for the future centered in a Messiah, who had been promised by almost all the prophets. After Malachi, as the years dragged on, the Jews scoured the scrolls of these prophets, seeking clues into their destiny. Of all the prophets, Isaiah gives perhaps the clearest picture of what the Jews might expect. His earlier messages blasted his nation's sin and unfaithfulness. But beginning with chapter 40, Isaiah shifts into a new key. Gone are the bleak predictions of judgment. Instead, a message of hope and joy breaks in. "Speak tenderly to Jerusalem, and proclaim to her that her hard service has been completed. . . ."

According to Isaiah, what happened to Judah was not God's defeat. God had in mind a new thing, a plan far more wonderful than anything seen before. In words that have become familiar, the book of Isaiah explains why the future holds hope—not just for the Jews, but for the whole world. A mysterious figure called "the servant" would, through his suffering, provide a means of rescue. Later, in a faraway time, God would usher in peace for all in a new heaven and new earth.

Chapter 40 introduces this last section of Isaiah with the sweeping declaration that God reigns over all. In many ways, these soaring words restate in global terms God's personal message to Job. "Surely the nations are like a drop in a bucket. . . . He sits enthroned above the circle of the earth, and its people are like grasshoppers." God shows himself master of nature, of history, indeed, of the entire universe.

LIFE QUESTION: *Why are there so many rhetorical questions in this chapter? What effect is the author trying to produce?*

Suffering Servant

*I*saiah's four songs about a "suffering servant" are among the richest, and most closely studied, passages in the Old Testament. The first part of the chapter stirs anticipation for a glorious time when God will restore Jerusalem and prove to all, "Your God reigns!" It looks like Israel will gain revenge on their enemies at last.

But the author explains how God will "redeem Jerusalem" by introducing the mysterious figure of the suffering servant, whose appearance was "disfigured beyond that of any man." Who is this suffering servant? And how will such a wounded person bring about a great victory?

Jewish scholars puzzled over these passages for centuries. What exactly did the prophet mean? Some of the servant songs refer to the nation of Israel as a whole, but passages like this one portray the servant as a specific individual, a great leader who suffers terribly. Although Isaiah holds him up as the deliverer of all humankind, he resembles more a tragic figure than a hero.

Some Jewish scholars speculated the prophet was describing himself or perhaps a colleague, such as Jeremiah. Still others focused their hopes on a Messiah to come. In general, however, the idea of the suffering servant never really caught on in the Jewish nation. They longed for a victorious Messiah, not a suffering one.

The image of the suffering servant went underground, lying dormant for centuries. Then, in a dramatic scene early in his ministry, Jesus quoted from one of Isaiah's servant passages. After reading aloud in the synagogue, Jesus "rolled up the scroll, gave it back to the attendant and sat down. The eyes of everyone in the synagogue were fastened on him, and he began by saying to them, 'Today this scripture is fulfilled in your hearing'" (Luke 4:20–21).

At last, a link snapped into place for some, but not all, of Jesus' listeners. The Messiah had come at last—not as a conquering general, but as a carpenter's son from Nazareth.

LIFE QUESTION: *If you had been a Jew in Jesus' day, would you have been disappointed in the Messiah?*

The Wounded Healer

KEY VERSE: *He was despised and rejected by men, a man of sorrows, and familiar with suffering. Like one from whom men hide their faces he was despised, and we esteemed him not. (Isa. 53:3)*

New Testament writers leave no doubt as to the identity of the suffering servant: at least ten times they apply Isaiah's four songs directly to Jesus. In one instance, Philip corrected an Ethiopian official who had wondered if the suffering servant referred to an ancient prophet (Acts 8:26–35).

Isaiah 53 reads almost like an eyewitness account of Jesus' last days on earth. The physical description—the Bible contains no other physical description of Jesus—is shocking. The servant "had no beauty or majesty to attract us to him"; he was "like one from whom men hide their faces." As this chapter foretells, Jesus did not open his mouth to answer his accusers at his trial. He left no descendants. He was cut off in the prime of life and, thanks to a gracious friend, was buried in a rich man's tomb. But that was not the end. After three days he saw "the light of life."

According to Isaiah, the servant died for a very specific purpose: "He was pierced for our transgressions." He took on pain for the sake of others, for *our* sakes. His wounds, an apparent defeat, made possible a great victory. His death sealed a future triumph when all that is wrong on earth will be set right. Significantly, the book of Isaiah does not end with the suffering servant image, but goes on to describe that wonderful life in a new heaven and new earth. But the time of travail was a necessary first step, for the servant absorbed in himself the punishment that was due for all the evils of the world.

Isaiah 53 forms an underlying foundation for much New Testament theology. In addition, these detailed prophecies, recorded many centuries before Jesus' birth, offer convincing proof that God was revealing his plan for the ages through the ancient prophets. He had not permanently severed his covenant with the Jews. Rather, out of Jewish roots—King David's own stock—he would bring forth a new king, a king like no other, to reclaim all the earth.

LIFE QUESTION: *Why did Jesus choose to come in the form described here?*

The End of It All

You will go out in joy and be led forth in peace; the mountains and hills will burst into song before you and all the trees of the field will clap their hands. (Isa. 55:12)

Isaiah had seen a glimpse of the future, and that glimpse convinced him that good news lay ahead. No invading armies, no terrible calamities could interfere with God's final purpose for the earth.

"For a brief moment I abandoned you, but with deep compassion I will bring you back," God says to Israel (54:7). Isaiah foretells a time when the ruined holy city, rebuilt, will achieve an unprecedented level of greatness. Yet the promise in these chapters goes far beyond what has ever been realized in Jerusalem. It merges into a vision of a future state where sin and sorrow no longer exist and we live in final peace with God.

The last part of Isaiah, addressed to a people facing deep despair, opens the door for the Jews to become a gift to all people. According to Isaiah, word about God will go out to nations nearby and faraway (66:18–21). This prophecy saw fulfillment in Jesus, who recruited disciples to carry his message worldwide. Through his life and death, the suffering servant indeed introduced the gospel to the entire world.

Whatever longings we feel on earth—for peace, for an end to suffering, for an unspoiled planet—will some day be fulfilled. Isaiah assures us that one day our very best dreams, all of them, will come true. We may not understand the process the world must go through to arrive at that future time, but, as this chapter makes clear, God's covenant with his people is everlasting. Nothing can cancel it.

As the decades, even centuries passed, empires—Babylon, Persia, Egypt, Greece, Syria, Rome—rose and fell, their armies chasing each other across the plains of Palestine. Each new empire subjugated the Jews with ease. Sometimes the entire race verged on extinction. Four centuries separate the last words of the prophets in the Old Testament and the first words of Matthew in the New Testament—"the 400 silent years," they are called. Did God care? Was he even alive? In desperation the common people waited for a Messiah; they had no other hope.

LIFE QUESTION: *What would you most like to see changed in the world? Does Isaiah speak to that change?*

A
Surprising
Messiah

Breakout

KEY VERSE:

But the angel said to her, "Do not be afraid, Mary, you have found favor with God. You will be with child and give birth to a son, and you are to give him the name Jesus."
(Luke 1:30–31)

*D*oes any human emotion run as deep as hope? Fairy tales, for example, pass down from generation to generation a belief in the impossibly happy ending, an irrepressible sense that in the end the forces of evil will lose the struggle and the brave and good will somehow triumph.

For the Jews in Palestine 2000 years ago, all hope seemed like a fairy tale. As Middle Eastern empires rose and fell, the tiny nation of Israel could never break free from the domination of greater powers. No prophet had spoken to them in 400 years. At the end of the Old Testament, God was in hiding. He had long threatened to hide his face, and as he did so a dark shadow fell across the planet.

For four centuries, the 400 years of God's silence, the Jews waited and wondered. God seemed passive, unconcerned, and deaf to their prayers. Only one hope remained, the ancient promise of a Messiah; on that promise the Jews staked everything. And then something momentous happened. The birth of a baby was announced—a birth unlike any that had come before.

You can catch the excitement just by watching the reactions of people in this chapter. The way Luke tells it, events surrounding Jesus' birth resembled a joy-filled musical. Characters crowded into the scene: a white-haired great uncle, an astonished virgin, a tottery old prophetess. They all smiled broadly and, as likely as not, burst into song. Once Mary overcame the shock from seeing an angel, she let loose with a beautiful hymn. Even an unborn cousin kicked for joy inside his mother's womb.

Luke takes care to make direct connections to Old Testament promises of a Messiah; the angel Gabriel even called John the Baptist an "Elijah" sent to prepare the way for the Lord. Clearly, something was brewing on planet earth. Among dreary, defeated villagers in a remote corner of the Roman Empire, something climactically good was breaking out.

LIFE QUESTION: *If an angel appeared to you, would you respond like Zechariah, or like Mary?*

God's Disguise

𝒩early every time an angel appears in the Bible, the first words he says are "Don't be afraid!" Little wonder. When the supernatural made contact with planet earth, it usually left the human observers flat on their faces, in catatonic fear. But Luke tells of God making an appearance on earth in a form that would not frighten. In Jesus, born in a barn and laid in a feeding trough, God found at last a mode of approach that we need not fear. What could be less scary than a newborn baby?

Imagine becoming a baby again: giving up language and muscle coordination, and the ability to eat solid food and control your bladder. That gives just a hint of the "emptying" that God went through.

According to the Bible, Jesus was both God and man. As God, he could work miracles, forgive sins, conquer death, and predict the future. Jesus did all that, provoking awe in the people around him. But for Jews accustomed to images of God as a bright cloud or pillar of fire, Jesus also caused much confusion. How could a baby in Bethlehem, a carpenter's son, a man from Nazareth, be the Messiah from God? Jesus' skin got in the way.

Puzzled skeptics would stalk Jesus throughout his ministry. But this chapter shows that God confirmed Jesus' identity from his earliest days. A group of shepherds in a field had no doubt—they heard the message of good news straight from a choir of angels. And an old prophet and prophetess recognized him also. Even the skeptical teachers in the temple were amazed.

Why did God empty himself and take on human form? The Bible gives many reasons, some densely theological and some quite practical. The scene of Jesus as an adolescent lecturing rabbis in the temple (2:41–5:2) gives one clue. For the first time, ordinary people could hold a conversation, a debate, with God in visible form. Jesus could talk to anyone—his parents, a rabbi, a poor widow—without first having to announce "Don't be afraid!" In Jesus, God came close.

LIFE QUESTION: *The scene of Jesus in the temple as a boy reveals a communication gap between Jesus and his parents. What other problems do you think he faced by being both God and man?*

Immediate Impact

The people were all so amazed that they asked each other, "What is this? A new teaching—and with authority! He even gives orders to evil spirits and they obey him." News about him spread quickly over the whole region of Galilee. (Mark 1:27–28)

𝒜lthough the four Gospels all cover basically the same ground, each one looks at Jesus' life from a unique angle. Matthew and Luke both begin with three chapters of historical background, taking pains to verify Jesus' Old Testament connections. Mark, however, plunges right in to report on Jesus' ministry, covering his baptism and temptation, the calling of the disciples, and a series of miracles in the first chapter alone.

Mark reads like a newspaper account, jam-packed with action, and with little room left over for parables, speeches, or editorial comments. Thus the book gives an ideal "bird's eye view" of Jesus' life. Its style—simple sentences without complicated transitions or long speeches—makes understanding easier.

After John the Baptist had fanned enthusiasm for Jesus—so much enthusiasm, in fact, that John landed in jail—Jesus openly announced his ministry. He had some surprises in store for the eager audience. For one thing, Jesus did not go to Jerusalem, the natural center of activity for any aspiring leader, but to the small towns in the hill country of Galilee. (He had grown up nearby, in the obscure town of Nazareth, which led some sophisticates to scoff, "Nazareth! Can anything good come from there?")

In other ways, too, Jesus did not fit the expected image of a prophet. His cousin John personified that severe ascetic image: He lived in a desert, ate insects, and preached a harsh message of judgment. But Jesus lived in the midst of people, dined in their homes, and brought a message of the good news of God.

When Jesus began healing people, however, his reputation swelled overnight. Mark shows gymnasium-size crowds pressing around Jesus so tightly that he had to plan escape routes. News of his miraculous powers spread even when he tried to hush it up. Wherever he went, the crowds followed, buzzing about his remarkable life. "Is he the Holy One of God?" "Is he mad?" "Isn't this the carpenter's boy?" The word was out.

LIFE QUESTION: *Based just on what you read in this chapter, what words would you use to describe Jesus?*

Signal Fires of Opposition

When a new leader starts making waves, opposition is sure to follow. While on earth, Jesus made an extravagant claim: He claimed to be the Messiah, sent from God. And opposition to him sprang up soon after the wild surge of popularity in Galilee. This chapter tells of three different criticisms that people would make against Jesus throughout his life.

He blasphemes. The teachers of the Law were scandalized by Jesus' forgiving sins. "Who can forgive sins but God alone?" they muttered. Jesus readily agreed that only God could forgive sins—that was his point exactly.

Throughout his life, Jesus faced strongest opposition from the most pious followers of Old Testament law. They could never accept that the awesome, distant God of Israel could take up residence inside a human body. Eventually, they had Jesus executed for making that claim. (People who accept Jesus as a "good man and enlightened teacher" today often overlook the scenes where Jesus blatantly identifies himself with God.)

He keeps disreputable company. Jesus showed a distinct preference for the most unseemly sort of people. Even after becoming famous he would dine with an outcast tax collector and his low-life friends. On hearing the gossip about this strange behavior, Jesus said simply, "It is not the healthy who need a doctor, but the sick. I have not come to call the righteous, but sinners."

He goes against tradition. To the Pharisees, it seemed Jesus' disciples were playing fast and loose with the holy Sabbath. Jesus' response: It's time for a new cloth; the old one has been patched together long enough. Before long, he would introduce the "new covenant." God had some major changes in store for the human race, and the narrow, confining covenant with the Israelites simply couldn't hold all those changes.

LIFE QUESTION: *Try to project yourself back into Jesus' time. What might have shocked you?*

Late-night Conversation

$\mathcal{R}$eading Mark 2 and John 3 back-to-back reveals a chief difference between Mark's and John's gospels. Mark gives the panoramic view: action, crowds, short scenes spliced together to create an overall impact. John tightens the camera angle, closing in on a few individual faces—a woman at a well, a blind man, a member of the Jewish ruling council—to compose a more intimate, in-depth portrait.

A simple word or phrase with a profound meaning—that is the style of Jesus' teaching as presented in John. No biblical author used simpler, more commonplace words: *water, world, light, life, birth, love, truth.* Yet John used them with such depth and skill that hundreds of authors since have tried to plumb their meaning.

Take this conversation with Nicodemus, for instance. He came to Jesus at night, in order to avoid detection. He risked his reputation and safety by even meeting with Jesus, whom his fellow Pharisees had sworn to kill. But Nicodemus had questions, burning questions, the most important questions anyone could ask: *Who are you, Jesus? Have you really come from God?* Jesus responded with the image of a second birth, in words we now recognize as among the most familiar in the Bible.

Evidently, some of Jesus' words to Nicodemus must have sunk in. Later he would stand up for Jesus at the Jewish ruling council and, after the crucifixion, help prepare Jesus' body for burial.

John follows this conversation with a report from John the Baptist. People were questioning him, too, about the new teacher across the river who was drawing all the crowds. In words that echo Jesus' own, John confirmed that Jesus held the keys to eternal life. He was indeed the one John had come to announce: "He must become greater; I must become less."

LIFE QUESTION: *How would you explain the phrase "born again" to someone who had never heard it?*

Miracles and Magic

Large crowds flocked from far away as word of Jesus' powers spread. Some people came for healing; others, just to witness the extraordinary phenomena. Who but a messenger from God could perform such works? Yet Jesus himself had an odd ambivalence toward miracles. He never did "tricks" on demand, like a magician. "A wicked and adulterous generation looks for a miraculous sign," he said to those who sought a display of magic (Matthew 12:39).

Jesus seemed not to trust miracles to produce the kind of faith he was interested in. Mark reports that on seven separate occasions he warned a person just healed, "Tell no one!" He was suspicious of the popular acclaim that his miracles stirred up, for he had a hard message of obedience and sacrifice, and miracles tended to attract gawkers and sensation-seekers.

Mainly, Jesus used his powers in compassionate response to human needs. Every time someone asked directly, he healed. When his disciples grew frightened on a stormy lake, he walked to them across the water or calmed the wind. When his audience got hungry he fed them, and when wedding guests grew thirsty he made wine.

Much like people today, Jesus' contemporaries looked for ways to explain away his powers, even when faced with irrefutable evidence. Here, for instance, the Pharisees seek to credit the miracles to Satan's power. On another occasion they arranged a formal tribunal, complete with judges and witnesses, to examine a man Jesus had healed. The man's parents confirmed his story ("One thing I do know. I was blind but now I see!"), but still the doubters hurled insults and threw him out of the court (John 9).

In short, the crowd's mixed responses bore out Jesus' suspicions about the limited value of miracles. They rarely created faith, but rather affirmed it in true seekers.

LIFE QUESTION: *Would people be more likely to believe God if miracles were more common today?*

Hard Soil

We who live 2000 years later, with events like Christmas and Easter marked plainly on our calendars, easily miss the sheer incredulity that greeted Jesus in the flesh.

Neighbors had watched him play in the streets with their own children; Jesus was simply too familiar for them to believe he was sent from God. "Isn't this the carpenter?" they asked. "Isn't this Mary's son and the brother of James, Joseph, Judas and Simon?" (Mark 6:3)

Not even Jesus' family could easily reconcile the wondrous and the ordinary. Mark casually mentions that one time Jesus' mother and brothers arrived to take charge of him because they had concluded, "He is out of his mind" (3:21). Neither could common people make up their minds about Jesus. They, too, judged him "raving mad" (John 10:20) one moment; then forcibly tried to crown him king the next.

The scribes and Pharisees, who pored over the prophets, should have had the clearest notion of what the Messiah would look like. But no group caused Jesus more trouble. They criticized his theology, his lifestyle, and his choice of friends. When he performed miracles, they attributed his power to Satan and demons.

When a storm nearly capsized the boat transporting Jesus, he yelled into the wind, "Quiet! Be still!" The disciples shrank back in terror. What kind of person could shout down the weather as if correcting an unruly child? That scene helped convince them Jesus was unlike anyone else on earth. Yet it suggests a reason for their confusion about him. Jesus had, after all, fallen asleep in the boat from fatigue, a symptom of his human frailty.

The early church argued for three centuries about exactly what happened when God became man, but their creeds did little to dispel the sense of mystery. In a way, Jesus was just like everyone else—he had a race, an occupation, a family background, a body shape. But, at the same time, he was something entirely new in the history of the universe. In between his humanity and deity lies the mystery that never completely goes away.

LIFE QUESTION: *In Jesus' story of the sower and the soil, what kind of "soil" best represents your own response to the gospel?*

Jesus and Illness

At one point some of the controversy about Jesus even affected John the Baptist, the prophet who more than anyone had raised the people's hopes about a Messiah. It was he who had baptized Jesus and pronounced him the Son of God. But two years later, as he languished on death row, John the Baptist himself began to wonder. He sent Jesus a direct question: "Are you the one who was to come, or should we expect someone else?"

Jesus replied: "Go back and report to John what you have seen and heard: The blind receive sight, the lame walk, those who have leprosy are cured, the deaf hear, the dead are raised, and the Good News is preached to the poor. Blessed is the man who does not fall away on account of me" (Luke 7:22–23). Clearly, Jesus saw his miracles of healing as important proofs of who he was.

The healings did something else as well: They overturned common notions about how God views sick people. At that time, the Pharisees taught a very strict principle that "All suffering comes from sin." They judged a deranged or demon-possessed person as permanently cursed by God. They saw God's hand of punishment in natural disasters, birth defects, and such long-term conditions as blindness and paralysis. Leprosy victims were unclean, excluded even from worship.

But Jesus contradicted such teaching. This chapter shows him curing a demon-possessed man, touching and healing an "unclean" woman, and resurrecting a child. On other occasions, he directly refuted the doctrine about sin and suffering. He denied that a man's blindness came from his own or his parents' sin, and he dismissed the common opinion that tragedies happen to those who deserve them (see John 9 and Luke 13).

Jesus did not heal everyone on earth, or even in Palestine. But his treatment of the sick and needy shows they are especially loved, not cursed, by God. The healings also provide a "sign" of what will happen in the future, when all diseases, and even death, will be destroyed.

LIFE QUESTION: *Do Christians around you still harbor the notion that a suffering person "got what he deserved"?*

Inflammatory Word

KEY VERSE: *For I tell you that unless your righteousness surpasses that of the Pharisees and the teachers of the law, you will certainly not enter the kingdom of heaven. (Matt. 5:20)*

If Jesus had avoided one emotionally charged word, *kingdom,* everything might have been different. Whenever he said it, images would dance in the minds of his audience: bright banners, glittering armies, the nation of Israel restored to glory. Jesus often used this word that quickened the pulse of Israel, starting with his first message, "Repent, for the kingdom of heaven is near" (4:17).

By boldly comparing himself to Solomon, Israel's most powerful king, Jesus tapped into the reservoir of his nation's deepest longings. More, he claimed that the promises of the prophets were coming true in him. What was about to happen, he said, was a new thing, and would far surpass anything from the past.

The expectations raised by such statements led to confusion and, finally, rejection. The initial excitement over Jesus' miracles was displaced by disappointment when he failed to restore the long-awaited kingdom. For, as it turned out, the word *kingdom* meant one thing to the crowd and quite another to Jesus.

Winds of change were blowing through Israel as Jesus spoke. Armed and well-organized, guerrilla fighters called Zealots were spoiling for a fight against oppressive Rome. But the signal for revolt never came. To their dismay, it gradually became clear that Jesus was not talking about a political or military kingdom.

Jesus indicated that we live in a visible world of families and people and cities and nations, "the kingdom of this world." But he called for people to commit their lives to an *invisible* kingdom, the "kingdom of heaven," more important and more valuable than anything in the visible world.

Success in the kingdom of heaven involves a great reversal of values, as seen in this major address, the Sermon on the Mount. "Blessed are the poor in spirit," Jesus said, and also those who mourn, and the meek, and those who hunger and thirst, and the persecuted . . . "for theirs is the kingdom of heaven." Status in this world is no guarantee of status in the kingdom of heaven.

LIFE QUESTION: *How does Jesus' formula for success compare with modern America's?*

Savings Account

KEY VERSE: *But seek first his kingdom and his righteousness, and all these things will be given to you as well. (Matt. 6:33)*

$\mathcal{M}$atthew 6, a continuation of the Sermon on the Mount, contains The Lord's Prayer, perhaps the most famous prayer of all. Jesus gave it as a model of prayer, and it captures well the message of the kingdom: "Your kingdom come, your will be done on earth as it is in heaven." Jesus sought to bring the two worlds together, and the Sermon on the Mount explains how.

At first glance, some of the advice may seem downright foolish: Give to everyone who asks, love your enemies, turn the other cheek, grant interest-free loans, don't worry about clothes or food. Can such idealism ever work in the "real," or visible, world? That was Jesus' point precisely: Break your obsession with safety, security, thriftiness, self-righteousness. Depend instead on the Father, letting him take care of the personal injustices that come your way, trusting him to look after your daily needs. In a nutshell, the message of the kingdom is this: Live for God and not other people.

The message applies to rewards as well. Most of us look to friends and colleagues for our rewards: a slap on the back, a hero medal, applause, a lavish compliment. But according to Jesus, by far the more important rewards await us after death. Therefore, the most significant human acts of all may be carried out in secret, seen by no one but God.

As Jesus explained it, we are accumulating a kind of savings account, "storing up treasures" in heaven rather than on earth. Treasures so great that they will pay back any amount of suffering in this life. The Old Testament had dropped a few scant hints about an afterlife, but Jesus spoke plainly about a place where "the righteous will shine like the sun in the kingdom of the Father" (13:43).

In their quest for a kingdom, the Jews had been looking for signs of God's approval in this life, primarily through prosperity and political power. Beginning with this speech, Jesus changed the focus to the life to come. He discounted success in this visible world. Invest in the future life, he cautioned; after all, rust, a thief, or a lowly insect can destroy all else that we accumulate.

LIFE QUESTION: *Of the people you know, who best puts these principles into practice?*

Kingdom Tales

*W*riters have long marveled at Jesus' skill in communicating profound truth through *parables*—short, simple, everyday stories with a moral.

The parables served Jesus' purposes perfectly. When he first told the stories in this chapter, he was floating offshore in a boat, shouting to the large crowds that had gathered. Because the stories concerned their daily lives—farming, baking bread, hunting buried treasure, fishing—he was able to hold their attention. And yet the parables simultaneously allowed Jesus to train his disciples "privately"; later on, he could take the disciples aside and explain the deeper meaning.

As Jesus told his disciples, parables also helped to winnow the audience. Spectators seeking entertainment could go home with a few stories to mull over, but more serious inquirers would need to come back for further interpretation. Parables also helped preserve his message: Years later, as people reflected on what Jesus taught, his parables came to mind in vivid detail.

Matthew 13 collects several of Jesus' stories about the "kingdom of heaven." Although Jesus never concisely defined the term, he gave many clues about the nature of his kingdom. Unlike, say, Greece or China or Spain, it has no geographical boundaries and can't be charted on a map. Its followers live right among their enemies, not separated from them by a moat or a wall. Still Jesus predicted that the kingdom would show remarkable growth even in an evil environment bent on its destruction.

In summary, the "kingdom of heaven" consists of the rule of God in the world. It comprises people of all races and from all nations who loyally follow God's will. The disciples, accustomed to more traditional images of power and leadership, couldn't quite grasp Jesus' concept of the kingdom. They kept asking him to explain his parables even as they jockeyed vainly for status. Not until he died, and then came back, did they comprehend his mission on earth.

LIFE QUESTION: *Jesus addressed peasants and fishermen. How would you express one of these parables in the terms of modern, technological society?*

Contrast in Power

KEY VERSE:

When Jesus landed and saw a large crowd, he had compassion on them, because they were like sheep without a shepherd. So he began teaching them many things. (Mark 6:34)

This chapter brings together scenes that illustrate very different kinds of power in the two kingdoms. Herod, ruler of Galilee, personified one kind. He was rich and ruthless, and had legions of Roman soldiers to carry out his every command. He left impressive monuments all over Palestine. Mark tells how Herod used power: He stole his brother's wife, locked up John the Baptist, and then had the prophet beheaded as a party trick. Killing John wasn't Herod's preference, but he felt the need to honor a careless vow in order to protect his image.

Jesus, too, was a leader—a king, in fact—but one who broke stereotypes. His power was undeniable; yet he used that power compassionately, to feed the hungry and heal the sick. At the beginning of his ministry, Jesus had declined a tempting offer of glory and territory, and after that he seemed to give no thought to cultivating an image of power or importance. He spent his time telling stories, not raising an army. He sought to please God, not to satisfy people's false expectations.

Herod had built a lavish palace in Jesus' home province of Galilee, but Jesus carefully avoided that fashionable area. As Herod wined and dined prominent guests in the resort town of Tiberias, Jesus roamed the countryside with his ragtag followers. He too served a banquet, of sorts, to 5000 unexpected guests. His simple message of love, forgiveness, and healing had its own kind of power. Mark tells of crowds chasing Jesus around a lake, running to fetch their sick friends, pressing in close to touch the Teacher.

Jesus had contemptuously dismissed Herod as "that fox." But as talk about Jesus spread, Herod longed for a chance to meet him. Eventually he got his chance, at Jesus' trial. Eager to see a miracle, Herod used charm, ridicule, and military force to try to coax some response from Jesus. He failed—Jesus never once succumbed to that kind of power.

LIFE QUESTION: *Which kind of power are most people attracted to? Which kind are you attracted to?*

Of Two Worlds

A story is told about Rabbi Joseph Schneerson, a Hasidic leader during the early days of the Russian revolution. The rabbi spent much time in jail, persecuted for his faith. One morning in 1927, as he prayed in a Leningrad synagogue, secret police rushed in and arrested him. They took him to a police station and worked him over, demanding that he give up his religious activities. He refused. The interrogator brandished a gun in his face and said, "This little toy has made many a man change his mind." Rabbi Schneerson answered, "This little toy can intimidate only that kind of man who has many gods and but one world. Because I have only one God and two worlds, I am not impressed by this little toy."

The theme of "two worlds," or two kingdoms, emerges often in Jesus' teaching, and two stories in this chapter draw a sharp distinction between the two worlds. "What is highly valued among men is detestable in God's sight," Jesus said, commenting on the first story. The second story, of the rich man and Lazarus, elaborates on that difference in values between the two worlds. The rich man prospered in this world, yet neglected to make any provision for eternal life and thus suffered the consequences. Meanwhile, a half-starved beggar, who by any standard would be judged a failure in this life, received an eternal reward.

Jesus told such stories to a Jewish audience with a tradition of wealthy patriarchs, strong kings, and victorious heroes. But Jesus kept emphasizing his stunning reversal of values. People who have little value in this world (the poor, the persecuted—people like Lazarus) may, in fact, have great stature in God's kingdom. Consistently he presented the visible world as a place to invest for the future, to store up treasure for the life to come.

Jesus once asked a question that brings the two worlds starkly together: "What good will it be for a man if he gains the whole world, yet forfeits his soul?" (Matthew 16:26).

LIFE QUESTION: *How would you rate yourself, using the standards of success and failure in this world? What if you used Jesus' standards?*

Jesus on Money

Jesus had more to say on money than almost any other topic. Yet two thousand years later, Christians have trouble agreeing on exactly what he *did* say. One reason is that he rarely gave "practical" advice. He avoided comment on specific economic systems and, as in this chapter, refused to get involved in personal disputes about finances. Jesus saw money primarily as a *spiritual* force.

One pastor boils down money issues into three questions: 1. How did you get it? (Did it involve injustice, cheating, oppression of the poor?) 2. What are you doing with it? (Are you hoarding it? Exploiting others? Wasting it on needless luxuries?) 3. What is it doing to you?

Although Jesus spoke to all three of those issues, he concentrated on the last one. As he explained it, money operates much like idolatry. It can catch hold and dominate a person's life, diverting attention away from God. Jesus challenged people to break free of money's power—even if it meant giving it all away.

This chapter offers a good summary of Jesus' attitude toward money. He did not condemn all possessions ("your Father knows that you need [food, drink, and clothes]"). But he strongly warned against putting faith in money to secure the future. As his story of the rich man shows, money will ultimately fail to solve life's biggest problems.

Jesus urged his listeners to seek treasure in the kingdom of God, for such treasure could benefit them in this life and the next one, too. "Do not worry," he said. Rather, trust God to provide your basic needs. To emphasize his point, he brought up the example of King Solomon, the richest man in the Old Testament. To most nationalistic Jews, Solomon was a hero, but Jesus saw him in a different light: Solomon's wealth had long since vanished, and even in his prime he was no more impressive than a common wildflower. Better to trust in the God who lavishes care on the whole earth than to spend your life worrying about money and possessions.

LIFE QUESTION: *How do you fit together Jesus' teaching and our culture's emphasis on financial security for the future?*

How to Succeed

KEY VERSE: *"I tell you the truth," Jesus said to them, "no one who has left home or wife or brothers or parents or children for the sake of the kingdom of God will fail to receive many times as much in this age and, in the age to come, eternal life." (Luke 18:29–30)*

𝒜 series of vignettes in this chapter reinforces the message about money, and about two worlds. In Luke's typical style, the stories feature underdogs: a mistreated widow, a despised tax collector, little children, a blind beggar. A rich man makes an appearance, but, like the rich man in the story of Lazarus, only as a negative example.

Even Jesus' closest disciples had trouble swallowing his teaching that money represents a grave danger. Yet Jesus sternly warned that wealth can keep people from the kingdom of God by tempting them to depend on themselves rather than on God. The story of the Pharisee and the tax collector expands that message. Not only wealth, but *any* form of pride or self-dependence tends to lead away from God.

An effort to become "holy," for example, may accomplish just the opposite if it results in spiritual pride and a feeling of superiority. Human beings have an incurable tendency to feed their own egos, to take credit, to compete. The way to God, said Jesus, is just the opposite: Trust God like a little child, admit wrong, let go.

Jesus reveals the key to true success in the very first story in this collection, a parable illustrating why we "should always pray and not give up." The persistent widow endured much frustration and apparent injustice before the judge finally granted her request. Similarly, Jesus implied, we may go through desert periods when it looks like God is ignoring our heartfelt requests. But in the end God himself will settle accounts. And all those whose faith holds firm, even in the hard times, will see justice.

LIFE QUESTION: *When have you resembled the Pharisee in Jesus' story? The tax collector?*

Responses
to Jesus

Master Storyteller

The chief priests, the teachers of the Law and the leaders among the people were trying to kill him. Yet they could not find any way to do it, because "all the people hung on his words" (Luke 19:47–48). Using simple, homespun images, Jesus expressed profound truths in a way that held his audience captive. His parables have won high praise even from literary experts who do not accept their message. Some of the most famous of these parables, including these three, appear only in Luke's gospel.

Although trained as a physician, Luke demonstrated great skill as a writer. The introduction to his book mentions that he carefully investigated reports from eyewitnesses before writing the book that bears his name. Using the finest Greek found in the New Testament, he brought characters and scenes vividly to life.

Luke especially excels at conveying the plight of the poor and the outcast. Women, largely ignored by ancient historians, play a large role in his book—he introduces thirteen mentioned nowhere else—as do children. It may seem strange that a man belonging to the upper class would emerge as a champion of the underdog—evidently, Jesus' own compassion had affected Luke deeply.

The three stories in this chapter all stir up feelings for the underdog. A shepherd scours the hillside in a frantic search for a missing sheep. A woman turns her house upside down over a lost silver coin. A runaway son thumbs his nose at a life of comfort and ends up half-starved in a pigpen. In a few brief sentences, the parables tug at feelings of loss and remorse that lie buried just beneath the surface in all of us. And yet all three parables end the same: Spectacular good news floods in to replace the sadness, and partying breaks out.

The word *gospel* itself comes from the Old English word *godspell*. It means, simply, "good news"—a message that Luke never lost sight of. Even for the saddest story, there can be a happy ending after all.

LIFE QUESTION: *In the story of the lost son, which of the two brothers do you most resemble?*

Food that Endures

KEY VERSE: *Whoever eats my flesh and drinks my blood has eternal life, and I will raise him up at the last day. . . . This is the bread that came down from heaven. Our forefathers ate manna and died, but he who feeds on this bread will live forever. (John 6:54, 58)*

*A*ll four Gospels include an account of the feeding of the 5000, but John adds the most detail. He describes the effect of the miracle on the ordinary people who saw it. At first, dazzled by the miracle, they tried to crown Jesus king. Characteristically, he slipped away, but the persistent crowd commandeered a few boats and sailed across a lake in pursuit.

The next day when the crowds caught up with him, Jesus met them with a blunt warning, "I tell you the truth, you are looking for me, not because you saw miraculous signs but because you ate the loaves and had your fill. Do not work for food that spoils, but for food that endures to eternal life, which the Son of Man will give you."

That response shows why Jesus distrusted sensation-seeking crowds: They cared far more for physical spectacle than for spiritual truth. And what happened next certainly bears out his suspicion. As he was interpreting the spiritual meaning of the miracle, all the enthusiasm of the previous day melted away. The crowd grew downright restless when he openly avowed his true identity as the one sent from God. They could not reconcile such exalted claims ("I have come down from heaven.") with their knowledge that he was a local man, whose mother and father they knew.

Jesus used the miracle they had seen firsthand as a way of introducing his topic of the bread of life (his words were later applied to the Lord's Supper). But in the end the crowd—who had proof of Jesus' supernatural power digesting in their bellies—abandoned him, unbelieving. Many of his disciples turned back too, never to follow him again.

LIFE QUESTION: *Why did the crowd take offense at Jesus? Why do people take offense at him today?*

Poles Apart

KEY VERSE: *You have let go of the commands of God and are holding on to the traditions of men. (Mark 7:8)*

Although the crowds sometimes had difficulty swallowing Jesus' message, they would tag along as long as he kept on healing people. On the other hand, the religious, political, and intellectual establishments all strongly opposed Jesus, but could not manage to loosen his grip upon the common people. The Pharisees, in particular, tried to trap him in a major blunder that might turn the people, or the government, against him.

In many ways, the Pharisees made for an odd set of enemies. They were, in fact, among the most religious people of Jesus' day. More than any other group, they strove to follow the letter of the Old Testament law. But Jesus could see right through the Pharisees' pious behavior. He blasted them for focusing on the "outside" while neglecting the far greater dangers from within.

Pharisees were strict legalists who proudly embellished Jewish law with their own traditions. For example, they determined that a person could ride a donkey without breaking the Sabbath rules, but not use a switch to speed up the animal. It was permissible to give to a beggar on the Sabbath only if the beggar stuck his hand inside the home, so the giver needn't reach outside. A woman could not look in the mirror on the Sabbath for she might see a gray hair and be tempted to pull it out.

Jesus reacted with surprising harshness to such seemingly petty matters. By concentrating on all the rules, the Pharisees risked missing the whole point of the gospel. Such external, showy forms of legalism did not get anyone closer to God; just the opposite, they tended to make people proud and cliquish and self-righteous.

One way Jesus exposed the hypocrisy in the Pharisees' attitude was by publicly healing people on the sacred Sabbath. Fully aware that such acts would scandalize strict Pharisees, he went ahead anyway, insisting that compassion for needy people must take precedence over any tradition.

LIFE QUESTION: *What Pharisee-like qualities exist in your church? In you?*

The Mathematics of Legalism

KEY VERSE: *"How many times shall I forgive my brother when he sins against me? Up to seven times?" Jesus answered, "I tell you, not seven times, but seventy-seven times." (Matt. 18:21–22)*

Although legalists, at first glance, may seem "righteous," Jesus warned against the subtle dangers of legalism. Oddly, it tends to lower a person's view of God. If I manage to meet all the requirements of a strict rule book, I may begin to feel secure about my own goodness. I may think that I have earned God's approval through my own efforts.

People who questioned Jesus in person—both his enemies the Pharisees and his friends the disciples—sought a precise list of rules so that they could strive to meet those obligations and thus feel satisfied. To such people, Jesus shouts a loud "No!" We never outgrow our need for God; we never *arrive* in the Christian life. We survive spiritually only if we constantly depend on God.

In the first story in this passage, Peter tries almost ludicrously to reduce forgiveness to a mathematical formula: *Let's see, exactly how many times must I forgive someone? Six? Seven?* Jesus mocks the question and tells a profound story about God's forgiveness, so all-encompassing that it defies all mathematics.

Next, the Pharisees try to pin down a formula for divorce. Once again Jesus avoids the answer they want to hear and points instead to the principles that undergird all marriages.

These examples illustrate how Jesus usually handled questions about specific problems. When a pious man asked which neighbors he should go about loving, Jesus told of the Good Samaritan who showed love even to his enemies. Jesus didn't tell a rich person to give away 18.5 percent of his belongings; he said to give them all away. He didn't restrict adultery to the act of intercourse; he connected it to lust, adultery of the heart. Murder? In principle, that's no different from anger.

In short, Jesus always refused to lower the sights. He lashed out at every form of legalism, every human attempt to accumulate a list of credits. The credit goes to God, not us. The chief danger facing legalists is that they risk missing the whole point of the gospel: It is a gift freely given by God to people who don't deserve it.

LIFE QUESTION: *When has it been hard for you to forgive someone?*

Coming Clean

KEY VERSE: Even though you do not believe me, believe the miracles, that you may know and understand that the Father is in me, and I in the Father. (John 10:38)

*E*very few years an author or movie director comes out with a new work raising questions about Jesus' identity. Often such portrayals show him wandering around the earth in a daze, trying to figure out why he came and what he is supposed to be doing. Nothing could be further from the account given us by John, Jesus' closest friend. According to him, Jesus was no "man who fell to earth," but God's Son, sent on a mission from the Father. "I know where I came from and where I am going," Jesus said (8:14).

Of the four gospel writers, John dwells most prominently on Jesus' identity as the true Messiah, the Son of God. He states his purpose in writing very clearly: "These are written that you may believe that Jesus is the Christ, the Son of God, and that by believing you may have life in his name" (20:31). His book includes incidents from no more than twenty days in Jesus' life, arranged so as to demonstrate who Jesus is. Significantly, most of these incidents come from the final days of Jesus' life, when he was declaring his mission openly.

"I am the gate," Jesus says in this chapter; "I am the good shepherd." Jews who heard those words undoubtedly thought back to Old Testament kings like David, who were known as the shepherds of Israel. When some challenged him bluntly, "If you are the Christ, tell us plainly," Jesus answered with equal bluntness, "I and the Father are one." The pious Jews understood him perfectly: They picked up stones to execute him for blasphemy.

Not even these hostile reactions surprised Jesus. He expected opposition, even execution. As he explained, a truly good shepherd, unlike a hired hand, "lays down his life for the sheep." He was the only person in history who chose to be born, chose to die, and chose to come back again. This chapter explains why he made those choices.

LIFE QUESTION: *What difference does it make that Jesus is God and not just a man?*

Turning Point

KEY VERSE: *"But what about you?" he asked. "Who do you say I am?" Peter answered, "You are the Christ." (Mark 8:29)*

As this chapter opens, Jesus is exasperated with his disciples. They had seen him feed 5000 people, and then 4000, and yet still they worried about their next meal. "Do you have eyes but fail to see, and ears but fail to hear?" he asked reproachfully. Still, for all their denseness, the disciples had grasped something about Jesus that eluded most others. The crowds saw him as a reincarnation of a prophet: Elijah, maybe, or John the Baptist. But in this scene, Peter boldly pronounces Jesus the "Christ," the very *Messiah* long predicted by the prophets.

It is difficult for us to comprehend the importance of that single word to first-century Jews. Ground down by centuries of foreign domination, they staked all their hopes in a *Messiah* who would lead their nation back to glory. Matthew records that Jesus, pleased by Peter's impulsive declaration, lavished praise on him (16:17–19). But, Peter's brightest moment was immediately followed by one of his dimmest—a few paragraphs later Jesus identifies Peter with Satan. What transpired between those two scenes marks an important turning point in the story of Jesus' life.

To Peter and the other disciples, "Messiah" stood for wealth and fame and political power. Jesus knew, though, that the true Messiah would first have to endure scorn, humiliation, suffering, and even death. He was the Suffering Servant prophesied by Isaiah. He would take up an executioner's cross, not a worldly position of honor.

Jesus accepted Peter's designation; he was indeed the true Messiah. But from that moment on, Jesus made a strategic shift. He left Galilee and headed toward the capital of Jerusalem. Instead of addressing the crowds, he narrowed his scope to the twelve disciples and worked to prepare them for the suffering and death to come. Peter may have grasped Jesus' identity, but he had much to learn about his mission. He wanted Jesus to avoid pain, not understanding that the pain of the cross would bring salvation to the whole world.

LIFE QUESTION: *If someone asked you who Jesus is, what would you say?*

Dull Disciples

KEY VERSE: *Jesus took Peter, James and John with him and led them up a high mountain, where they were all alone. There he was transfigured before them. (Mark 9:2)*

Despite the increased attention, Jesus' closest disciples, the Twelve, did not distinguish themselves—to put it midly. "Are you so dull?" Jesus asked them at one point, and later sighed in exasperation, "How long shall I put up with you?" This chapter alone shows the disciples bungling a work of healing, misunderstanding Jesus' hints about his coming death and resurrection, squabbling about status, and trying to shut down the work of another disciple. Obviously, there was much in Jesus' mission they failed to comprehend.

Three of the disciples observed a dramatic scene that should have quelled any lingering doubts. "The Transfiguration," reported in vivid detail by Matthew, Mark, and Luke, afforded absolute proof of God's approval. Jesus' face shone like the sun and his clothes became dazzling, "whiter than anyone in the world could bleach them." A cloud enveloped the disciples and inside that cloud, to their astonishment, they found two long-dead giants of Jewish history: Moses and Elijah. It was too much to take; when God spoke audibly in the cloud, the disciples fell down, terrified. (Most scholars believe Mark got his details from Peter, one of the eyewitnesses, who describes the long-term impact of this experience in 2 Peter 1:16–18.)

Yet what effect did such a stupendous event have on the disciples? Did it permanently silence their questions and fill them with solid faith? A few weeks later, each one of the Twelve—including the three eyewitnesses of the Transfiguration—abandoned Jesus in his hour of deepest need. Somehow the import of who Jesus was, God in flesh, never really sank in until after he had left and then come back.

Actually, the fact of the disciples' abrupt change makes compelling evidence for Jesus' resurrection. The cowering disciples portrayed in Mark hardly resemble the bold, confident figures in the book of Acts. Something incredible had to happen to turn this bunch of bumblers into heroes of the faith.

LIFE QUESTION: *This chapter includes both "highs" and "lows" in the disciples' experience. What would a graph of your spiritual journey look like?*

Mission Improbable

Jesus' time on earth was running out. Only a few weeks remained for him to prepare others to carry on his work, and he used that time for a crash training course. In this chapter Jesus advances his plan of "turning over" his work to his followers. This time he commissioned seventy-two, not twelve, followers in a hazardous assignment.

A seismic change was rumbling. As Jesus described their mission, he did not disguise his alarm. "Go! I am sending you out like lambs among wolves," he said. Finally, in a voice that commanded attention, he gave this mysterious charge: "He who listens to you listens to me; he who rejects you rejects me."

Luke's next view of Jesus is almost unprecedented in the Gospels. Nowhere else will you find Jesus so happy, so bubbling with joy. The caution in his face had turned to exuberance. It had really worked, the dangerous mission into the hill country, and Jesus celebrated the enormous breakthrough with those seventy-two disciples.

In that triumphant response Jesus reveals the significance of the final days of his mission. He had come to earth to establish a *church,* a group of people who would carry on his will after his departure. And while those seventy-two disciples were plodding the dusty roads of Judea, knocking on doors, explaining the Messiah, Jesus watched Satan fall like lightning from heaven. Their actions won a cosmic victory. Jesus' own mission, his own life, was being lived out through seventy-two very ordinary human beings.

The sending of the seventy-two disciples is only one of three stories in this rich chapter. Taken together, the three provide a full picture of what following Jesus might include. For the seventy-two, it meant boldly proclaiming the kingdom of God; for the Good Samaritan, it meant binding the wounds of a robbery victim; for Mary, it meant total absorption in the words of Jesus.

LIFE QUESTION: *Of the three ways of following Jesus described in this chapter, which do you do best?*

Servant Leadership

This scene opens with yet another prediction of Jesus' death. Showing incredible insensitivity, two of the disciples immediately lapsed into a petty dispute about status. They could not grasp the message Jesus patiently repeated for them: In his kingdom, the greatest is the one who *serves*.

Jesus used curious techniques to gain recruits for his kingdom. His job descriptions included such words as "cross" and "slave"—rather like a Marine Corps recruiter displaying photos of war amputees and dead soldiers. Not even his closest friends could comprehend how the ugly image of an executioner's cross fit their dreams of a new kingdom. No matter how many times Jesus explained the way of the cross, it never seemed to sink in.

As the group reached Jerusalem, however, Jesus did permit one great display of public adulation. Always before, he had shrunk away from the crowds who tried to coronate him. But in the "triumphal entry" of Palm Sunday he let people honor him as the conquering Messiah.

In some ways, the procession was a slapstick affair compared to the lavish processions of the Romans—Jesus rode on a donkey, after all, not on a stallion or in a gilded chariot. But the event, foretold by the prophets, had deep meaning for the Jews. Jesus was openly declaring himself as Messiah, and the triumphal entry set all of Jerusalem astir.

Jewish leaders who opposed Jesus raised an alarm, and even the Romans took note of a man claiming to be a king. The rest of the Gospels, however, demonstrate how tragically short-lived Jesus' public acceptance proved to be. The crowds, like the disciples, were wholly unprepared for Jesus' style of kingdom. Its demands were too hard; its rewards too vague.

LIFE QUESTION: *How can a person demonstrate "servant leadership" today?*

161

Opposition Heats Up

The last few weeks of Jesus' life show a mounting sense of urgency, as seen in several dramatic confrontations at the temple. That sacred site, supposedly the center for worship of God, had taken on a commercial cast. Merchants, who sold sacrificial animals to pilgrims and foreigners at inflated prices, seemed more interested in profit than in true worship. In the spirit of the Old Testament prophets, Jesus branded them "robbers" and forcibly drove them out.

Mark folds that scene into an account of a fig tree cursed by Jesus because of its lack of fruit. He was probably drawing a direct parallel to the religious establishment of the day. It, too, was "withered," and Jesus was about to take decisive action against it.

Jesus did nothing to temper his harsh message. On the contrary, he told a parable that seemed deliberately provocative. He presented himself as God's last resort, his final attempt to break through stubborn resistance. But he, too, would be killed, by the same people whose ancestors had mocked and killed the prophets.

Battle lines were drawn. On one side was Jesus, kept safe only by his widespread popularity. On the other were leaders of the religious and political establishments. Threatened by Jesus' radical message of repentance and reform, they determined to find a way to trap Jesus and turn the crowd against him.

LIFE QUESTION: *How would you label Jesus' primary emotion in each of the stories of this passage?*

Mark 12:13–44

Baiting Jesus

KEY VERSE: *They came to him and said, . . . "Is it right to pay taxes to Caesar or not?" Then Jesus said to them, "Give to Caesar what is Caesar's and to God what is God's." (Mark 12:14, 17)*

Mark 12 records three different skirmishes between Jesus and the groups seeking to trap him.

The Pharisees, allied with a party following Herod, cynically praised Jesus, and then sprang on him a double-bind question: "Is it right to pay taxes to Caesar or not?" If Jesus said "Pay the taxes," he would lose popular support, for the independence-minded Jews despised Roman occupation forces. If he said "Don't pay," he could be turned in to Rome for breaking the law.

Next, a small but powerful religious group tried to stump Jesus with a theological question. The Sadducees, who did not believe in an afterlife, proposed a complicated riddle about life after death.

Finally, Jesus' perennial enemies the Pharisees took their turn. Jewish rabbis counted 613 commandments in the Law, and various splinter groups bickered over which ones were most important. The teacher of the Law asked Jesus to select just one as the greatest commandment of all, knowing his choice would offend some of those groups.

Jesus avoided each of the verbal traps, succeeding so brilliantly that Mark concludes, "And from then on no one dared ask him any more questions." In all these skirmishes, Jesus did not try to placate his adversaries. Instead, he used the occasions of conflict to warn his disciples and the watching crowds against those adversaries, whose fury only increased.

After he had fended off the last critic, Jesus pointed to a poor widow who had just made a tiny but sacrificial offering for the temple treasury. Her faithfulness, said Jesus, was far more impressive than that of the greedy religious establishment, who "devour widows' houses and for a show make lengthy prayers."

LIFE QUESTION: *What can you learn from Jesus' style in handling his enemies? How do you tend to respond to people who oppose you?*

A Day to Dread

Move forward a few days, beyond the events of this chapter, as Jesus is prodded by Roman soldiers toward the place of execution. A group of women follows behind, hysterical with grief. Suddenly Jesus turns and silences them with these words, "Daughters of Jerusalem, do not weep for me; weep for yourselves and for your children. . . . For if men do these things when the tree is green, what will happen when it is dry?" (Luke 23:28, 31).

Even in Jesus' childhood, rumors about him had provoked a king's bloody campaign of infanticide. And as this chapter spells out in grim detail, Jesus did not expect the war against God's kingdom to end with his own death. He predicted that evil would only intensify until at last, in one final spasm of rebellion, the earth would give way to God's restoration.

"Before we can hear the last word," said Dietrich Bonhoeffer, "we must listen to the next-to-the-last word," and in the Bible that consists of dreadful apocalyptic visions. At the end of time, God will take off all the wraps. And when Jesus returns, he will appear in a new form—not as a helpless babe in a manger, not nailed to a crosspiece of wood, but as "the Son of Man coming in clouds with great power and glory."

Some of Jesus' dire predictions found fulfillment in A.D. 70, when Roman soldiers broke through the walls of Jerusalem and demolished Herod's temple. Other predictions, clearly, have not yet been fulfilled. In this passage, Jesus gives direct clues to events that will precede his second coming. But he ends with a warning that no one can calculate the precise time of his return to earth.

It didn't take long for doubters to appear on the scene. Just a few decades later scoffers were already mocking the notion of the "second coming" of Christ. "Where is this 'coming' he promised? . . . everything goes on as it has since the beginning of creation" (2 Peter 3:4). For all such scoffers, Jesus and the prophets have one ominous word of advice: Just wait. God will not remain silent forever. One day, earth and sky will flee from his presence.

LIFE QUESTION: *What response did Jesus want from the disciples who first heard these words? What response does he want from us?*

A Scent of Doom

The Passover, an annual commemoration of the Israelites' deliverance from Egypt, was one of the high points of the Jewish calendar. All males older than twelve traveled to Jerusalem for the holiday, filling the city with hundreds of thousands of pilgrims.

Jesus had entered that festive scene in a moment of triumph on Palm Sunday, but very soon a sense of doom stole in. He seemed obsessed with death. When a woman splashed him with expensive perfume, he called it a form of burial preparation.

Passover festivities culminated in a solemn meal, where family and close friends gathered to remember the Exodus, the time of liberation. They tasted morsels of food, sipped wine, and read aloud the stories from the Old Testament. They also selected a lamb to take to the temple and offer as a sacrifice to God. Thus, the holiday ended on a sad and bloody note.

Outside the room, Jesus' enemies were stalking, waiting for an occasion to seize him. Inside, the disciples swore loyalty to their leader, even as he insisted that, down to a man, all would soon forsake him. It was at this somber meal that Jesus made a profound declaration. "This is the blood of the new covenant," he said as he poured the wine. "Take it, this is my body," he said, breaking bread.

What the disciples did not fully understand was that a dream was dying—a dream of a mighty nation, God's covenant nation. Jesus was announcing a new covenant, sealed not with the blood of lambs, but with his own blood. The new kingdom, the kingdom of God, would not be led by Jewish generals and kings, but rather by the scared band of disciples gathered around the table—the very disciples who would soon betray him.

Today, virtually all Christian churches continue the practice of Communion (Mass, Eucharist, or Lord's Supper) in some form. That solemn ceremony dates back to this original Passover meal when Jesus instituted the new covenant.

LIFE QUESTION: *How does the tone of the Lord's Supper in your church resemble, or differ from, this original scene?*

165

Final
Days

One Final Meal Together

The apostle John devoted one-third of his gospel to the last twenty-four hours of Jesus' life. John stretched The Passover meal out over five chapters (13–17), and nothing like these chapters exists elsewhere in the Bible. Their slow-motion, realistic detail provides an intimate memoir of Jesus' most anguished evening on earth.

Leonardo da Vinci immortalized the setting of The Last Supper in his famous painting, arranging the participants on one side of the table as if they were posing for the artist. John avoids physical details and presents instead the maelstrom of human emotions. He holds a light to the disciples' faces, and you can almost see the awareness flickering in their eyes. All that Jesus had told them over the past three years was settling in.

Never before had Jesus been so direct with them. It was his last chance to communicate to them the significance of his life and his death. He refrained from parables and painstakingly answered the disciples' redundant questions. The world was about to undergo a convulsive trauma, and the eleven fearful men with him were his hope for that world.

"I am going away, and I am coming back to you," Jesus kept repeating, until at last the disciples showed signs of comprehension. God's Son had entered the world to reside in one body. He was now leaving earth to return to the Father. But someone else—the Spirit of truth, the Counselor—would come to take up residence in many bodies, in *their* bodies.

Jesus was planning to die, yes. He was leaving them. But in some mysterious way, he was not leaving. He would not stay dead. That night, Jesus gave them an intimacy with the Father such as they had never known; yet he promised an even greater intimacy to come. He seemed aware that much of what they nodded their heads at now would not sink in until later.

LIFE QUESTION: *This chapter contains many promises. Which have been fulfilled in your life?*

The Vital Link

The sense of urgency grew inside the stuffy, crowded room. Jesus had just a few more hours to prepare his disciples for the tumult that lay ahead. More, they were his closest friends in all the world, and he was about to leave them.

In this passage, Jesus envisions what will happen to the little band after his departure. He foresees fierce opposition, and hatred, and beatings, and executions. The disciples would face all these trials on his behalf, and without his physical presence to protect them.

As he had done so often, Jesus searched for an allegory, a parable from nature to drive home his point. Just outside Jerusalem, rows of vineyards covered the hills—probably, he and his disciples had walked through them on their way to the city—and Jesus summoned up two images from those vineyards.

First, the image of lush, juicy grapes. Not long before, the disciples had drunk the product of those grapes as they listened to Jesus' deeply symbolic words about the blood of the covenant. In order to bear fruit, Jesus said, one thing was essential: They must remain in intimate connection with the vine. Jesus also reminded the Twelve that he had handpicked them for a specific mission: "to go and bear fruit—fruit that will last."

Then Jesus mentioned one more image: a pile of dead sticks at the edge of the vineyard. Somehow, these branches had lost their connection with the vine, the source of nourishment. A farmer had snapped them off and thrown them in a heap for burning. They no longer had a useful function.

Most likely, Jesus' disciples did not fully understand his meaning that night. But the symbol, with its abrupt contrast between juicy grapes and withered branches, would stay with them. The spectacular history of the early church gives certain proof that they eventually heeded his heartfelt words about "remaining" in him.

LIFE QUESTION: *In what ways do you work at "remaining" in Jesus?*

Turning Bad into Good

I have told you these things, so that in me you may have peace. In this world you will have trouble. But take heart! I have overcome the world. (John 16:33)

*A*fter the allegory of the vine and branches, Jesus turned from word pictures and spoke directly about what would happen to the disciples. Never was he more "theological" with them. Some of it they understood; some of it they did not. John shows them whispering to each other, trying to figure out his meaning.

Perhaps the strangest words of all were these: "It is for your good that I am going away." Good? How could it possibly be good for him to abandon them, thus dashing their hopes of a restored kingdom? Jesus tried to explain the advantages to come, when the Spirit would live inside them, but the disciples were too busy discussing what he meant by "going away" to comprehend.

Jesus' analogy of childbirth gave a further clue. Although childbirth may involve great pain, the pain is not a dead end, like pain caused by cancer. The effort of giving birth produces something—new life!—and results in joy. In the same way, the great sorrow he and the disciples were about to undergo would not be a dead end. His pain would bring about the salvation of the world; their grief would turn to joy.

Jesus concluded his words that fateful evening with a ringing declaration, "Take heart! I have overcome the world." How hollow this statement would seem the next evening when his pale, abused body hung on an executioner's cross, and the disciples slunk away in the darkness. Their emotions, and faith, were to rise and plummet in one unforgettable day—just as Jesus had predicted in his analogy of childbirth.

LIFE QUESTION: *How would the world be different if Jesus had stayed on earth instead of going away?*

Commissioning

*W*hen the disciples responded to Jesus' speech with the bold pronouncement, "This makes us believe that you came from God," it seemed to settle something in Jesus' mind. "You believe at last!" he said, with obvious relief, and then concluded the intimate get-together with this, his longest recorded prayer. In it, Jesus summed up his feelings and his plans for the tight circle of friends gathered around him.

Their previous missions, the preaching and healing ministries in the countryside, had been mere warm-up exercises. Now he was turning everything over to them. "I confer on you a kingdom, just as my Father conferred one on me," he said (Luke 22:29). His prayer represented a kind of commissioning or graduation.

Using language full of mystery, Jesus told them that he must leave the world but they must remain in it to proclaim him. They would now attract the hatred and hostility that had previously been directed against him. And yet, although they lived "in the world," they were not quite "of the world." Something set them apart from the world and bound them together with him in unity with God— a unity so close as to defy all explanation.

Jesus prayed, too, for the other believers who would follow them, stretching in an unbroken chain throughout history. "I pray . . . that all of them may be one, Father, just as you are in me and I am in you. May they also be in us so that the world may believe that you have sent me." And then he led the frightened little band to his appointment with death.

LIFE QUESTION: *Based on this prayer, how would you sum up Jesus' goals for the church? How well does your church fulfill those goals?*

Appointment with Destiny

As Jesus prayed in Gethsemane, a quiet, cool grove of olive trees, while three of his disciples waited sleepily outside, a large armed mob made its way toward the garden to seize and torture Jesus.

He felt afraid, and abandoned. Falling facedown on the ground, he prayed for some way out. The future of the human race and of the entire universe came down to this one weeping figure. His sweat fell to the ground in large drops, like blood.

All the deep ironies of Jesus' life came crashing together that evening in the garden when the one whom wise men had crossed a continent to worship was sold, like a slave, for thirty pieces of silver. Jesus' disciples still had not come to terms with the kind of "kingdom" Jesus wanted to establish. Blustery Peter was prepared to install a kingdom the traditional way—by force. When Peter hacked off a guard's ear, however, Jesus stopped the violence and performed, notably, his last miracle: He healed the guard.

With a single prayer, Jesus reminded his friends, he could dispatch squadrons of angels. He had the power to defend himself, but he would not use it. When the disciples realized that they could expect no last-minute rescue operations from the invisible world, they all fled. If Jesus would not protect himself, how could he protect them?

Matthew's account of what transpired in Gethsemane and before the Sanhedrin shows that, in an odd inversion, the "victim" dominated all that took place. Jesus, not Judas, not the mob, and not the high priest, acted like one truly in control. When they put him on the stand and accused him, he maintained a regal silence. "Tell us if you are the Christ [Messiah], the Son of God," they demanded. He finally answered with a simple "Yes, it is as you say."

That single admission condemned Jesus to death, for the Sanhedrin had a different expectation of the Messiah. They wanted a conqueror to set them free by force. Jesus knew that only one thing—his death—would truly set them free. For that reason he had come to earth.

LIFE QUESTION: *If you had been in the garden with Jesus, how would you have reacted to the scene of confrontation?*

No Justice

KEY VERSE: *When the crowd had gathered, Pilate asked them, "Which one do you want me to release to you: Barabbas, or Jesus who is called Christ?" (Matt. 27:17)*

The Gospels record a pass-the-buck sequence in Jesus' encounter with "justice." Roman law had granted the Jews many freedoms, including the right to their own court system, the Sanhedrin. When Jesus identified himself as the Messiah, the Sanhedrin convicted him of the religious charge of blasphemy, a capital offense. However, the Sanhedrin had no authority to carry out a death sentence; that required the sanction of Roman justice. Thus Jesus' opponents sent him to Pilate, the Roman governor of Judea.

Along the way, the accusers changed the charge against Jesus from a religious one (which would not have impressed Pilate) to a political one. They portrayed Jesus as a dangerous revolutionary who had declared himself king of the Jews in defiance of Roman rule. Pilate had grave misgivings about the charge, and his wife's premonitions compounded his sense of uneasiness.

Luke records that Pilate at first declared Jesus innocent despite pressure from the crowd. Then he sought a way out of his dilemma by deferring the case to Herod, who had jurisdiction over Jesus' home region. Herod, disappointed by Jesus' silence and his refusal to perform miracles, ultimately sent him back to Pilate.

As Pilate tried three times to get the Jewish leaders to release their prisoner, the fury of the crowd against Jesus swelled. At last, facing a mob scene, the canny governor yielded to their demands, but only after ceremoniously washing his hands of innocent blood.

Through all these legal proceedings, Jesus kept an almost unbroken silence. He was acknowledged king at last—with a crown of thorns jammed onto his head, and a royal robe draped across his bloodied back. Pilate seemed to recognize, at some level, the enormity of the injustice he had participated in. He prepared a notice of Jesus' "crime" to be fastened to the cross, which read, in three languages, "JESUS OF NAZARETH, THE KING OF THE JEWS." When the chief priests protested that it should read only that Jesus *claimed* to be king, Pilate answered, "What I have written, I have written" (John 19).

LIFE QUESTION: *What was it about Jesus that stirred up such strong feelings in his opponents?*

The Last Temptation

KEY VERSE: *With a loud cry, Jesus breathed his last. The curtain of the temple was torn in two from top to bottom. (Mark 15:37–38)*

Long before, at the very beginning of his ministry, Jesus had resisted Satan's temptation toward an easier path of safety and physical comfort. Now, as the moment of truth drew near, that temptation must have seemed more alluring than ever.

On the cross, a criminal at Jesus' left taunted him, "Aren't you the Christ? Then save yourself and us." The crowd milling about took up the cry: "Let him come down from the cross, and we will believe in him. . . . Let God rescue him now if he wants him."

But there was no rescue, no miracle. There was only silence. The Father had turned his back, or so it seemed, letting history take its course, letting everything evil in the world triumph over everything good. How could Jesus save others when, quite simply, he could not save himself?

Why did Jesus have to die? Theologians who ponder such things have debated various theories of "the Atonement" for centuries, with little agreement. Somehow it required love, sacrificial love, to win what could not be won by force.

One detail Mark includes may provide a clue. Jesus had just uttered the awful cry, "My God, my God, why have you forsaken me?" He, God's Son, identified so closely with the human race— taking on their sin!—that God the Father had to turn away. The gulf was that great. But, just as Jesus breathed his last, "The curtain of the temple was torn in two from top to bottom."

That massive curtain served to seal off the Most Holy Place, where God's Presence dwelled. No one except the high priest was allowed inside, and he could enter only once a year, on a designated day. As the author of Hebrews would later note, the tearing of that curtain showed beyond doubt exactly what was accomplished by Jesus' death on the cross. No more sacrifices would ever be required. Jesus won for all of us—ordinary people, not just priests—immediate access to God's presence. By taking on the burden of human sin, and bearing its punishment, Jesus removed forever the barrier between God and us.

LIFE QUESTION: *When have you most wanted a "miracle" in your life and been disappointed? What did you learn from that experience?*

Signs of Life

When the greatest miracle of all history occurred, the only eyewitnesses were soldiers standing guard outside Jesus' tomb. When the earth shook and an angel appeared, bright as lightning, these guards trembled and became like dead men. Then, with an incurably human reflex, they fled to the authorities to report the disturbance.

But here is an astounding fact: Later that afternoon the soldiers, who had seen proof of the Resurrection with their own eyes, changed their story. The resurrection of the Son of God did not seem nearly as significant as, say, stacks of freshly minted silver.

A few women, grieving friends of Jesus, were next to learn of the Miracle of Miracles. Matthew reports that when an angel broke the news of Jesus' resurrection, the women hurried away "afraid yet filled with joy." *Fear,* the reflexive human response to a supernatural encounter—when the women heard from a glowing angel firsthand news of an event beyond comprehension, of course they felt afraid. *Yet filled with joy*—the news they heard was the best news of all, news too good to be true, news so good it had to be true. Jesus was back! He had returned, as promised. The dreams of the Messiah all came surging back as the women ran fearfully and joyfully to tell the disciples.

Even as the women ran, the soldiers were rehearsing an alibi, their part in an elaborate cover-up scheme. Like everything else in Jesus' life, his resurrection drew forth two contrasting responses. Those who believed were transformed, finding enough hope and courage to go out and change the world. But those who chose not to believe found ways to ignore evidence they had seen with their own eyes.

LIFE QUESTION: *What makes you believe, or not believe, in Jesus?*

The Rumor Confirmed

People who discount the Resurrection tend to portray the disciples as gullible country bumpkins with a weakness for ghost stories, or as shrewd conspirators who hatch a resurrection plot to attract popular support for their movement. The Bible presents a radically different picture. It shows Jesus' followers themselves as the ones most skeptical of rumors about a risen Jesus.

Reports from the women of an empty tomb failed to convince the disciples, so Peter and another ran to the graveyard to see for themselves. That same night the disciples huddled in a locked room, afraid of the Jewish leaders, apparently still skeptical.

For his part, Jesus went out of his way to allay the disciples' fears and suspicions. In broad daylight he visited and fished with them. Once he asked a dubious Thomas to test his scarred skin by touch. Another time he ate a piece of broiled fish in their presence to prove he was not a ghost (Luke 24). This was no mirage, no hallucination; it was Jesus their master, no one else.

The appearances of the risen Christ recorded in the Bible, fewer than a dozen, show a clear pattern. With one exception, he visited small groups of people closeted indoors or in a remote area. By the garden tomb, in a locked room, on the road to Emmaus, beside the Sea of Galilee, atop the Mount of Olives—such private encounters bolstered the faith of people who already believed in Jesus. But as far as we know, not a single unbeliever saw Jesus after his death.

What would have happened if Jesus had reappeared on Pilate's porch or before the Sanhedrin, this time with a withering blast against those who had ordered his death? Surely such a public scene would have caused a sensation. But would it have kindled faith? Jesus had already answered that question in his story of Lazarus and the rich man: "If they do not listen to Moses and the Prophets, they will not be convinced even if someone rises from the dead" (Luke 16). Instead, Jesus chose another way: to let the disciples themselves spread the word, as his witnesses.

LIFE QUESTION: Would you have greeted the news of Jesus' resurrection like Mary? Like Peter? Like Thomas?

Roadside Encounter

KEY VERSE: *Then their eyes were opened and they recognized him, and he disappeared from their sight. (Luke 24:31)*

In this scene at the end of Luke's gospel, two followers were walking away from Jerusalem, downhearted and perplexed. Their dream of "the one who was going to redeem Israel" had died along with their leader on the cross. And yet they too had heard the crazy rumors of an empty tomb. What did it all mean?

A stranger appeared beside the two forlorn disciples. At first he seemed the only man alive who hadn't heard about the incredible week in Jerusalem. But as he talked it became clear that he knew more about what had happened than anyone. Painstakingly, he traced the whole story of the gospel, beginning with Moses and the prophets. According to him, the prophets had predicted all along that the Messiah would suffer these things.

The stranger fascinated them, so much so that they begged him to stay longer. Then at mealtime, he made a hauntingly familiar gesture and the last link snapped into place. It was Jesus sitting at their table! No one else. Without a doubt, he was alive.

They were two ordinary people, but the encounter with the risen Christ changed them forever. "Were not our hearts burning within us while he talked with us on the road and opened the Scriptures to us?" they recalled. They dashed to meet the Twelve (now Eleven, with Judas's betrayal) only to learn that Peter, too, had seen Jesus. Suddenly, in the midst of that chaotic scene of joy and confusion, Jesus himself appeared. He explained once and for all that his death and resurrection were not unforeseen, but rather lay at the heart of God's plan all along.

Jesus had one last promise to keep: He departed from earth, and in his place left the band of believers to carry out his mission. These people, common people with more than a touch of cowardice, had followed Jesus, listened to him, and watched him die. But seeing Jesus alive changed all that. They returned to Jerusalem with great joy, and before long they were out telling the world the good news.

LIFE QUESTION: *How did the truth about Jesus "dawn" on you?*

The Word Spreads

Departed, But Not Gone

The disciples' obsession with Israel's restored kingdom did not fade even after Jesus had died and come back to life. For forty days after the Resurrection he appeared and disappeared seemingly at will. When he came, his followers listened eagerly to his explanations of all that had happened. When he left, they plotted the structure of the new kingdom that he would surely inaugurate. Think of it: Jerusalem free at last from Roman domination.

Jesus gave some mystifying orders, however. He told his followers to return to Jerusalem and simply wait. Something more was needed. Do not leave the city, he said, until the Holy Spirit comes. At last, one of the disciples put to Jesus the question they had all been debating together, "Lord, are you at this time going to restore the kingdom to Israel?"

No one was prepared for Jesus' reaction. He seemed to brush the question aside, deflecting attention away from Israel toward neighboring countries, all the way to the ends of the earth. He mentioned the Holy Spirit again, and then, to everyone's utter amazement, his body lifted off the ground, suspended there for a moment, then disappeared into a cloud. And they never saw him again.

Christians believe that all of history revolves around the life of Jesus the Christ. But the plain fact is that Jesus left earth after thirty-three years. Furthermore, he declared it a good thing: "You are filled with grief. But I tell you the truth: It is for your good that I am going away. Unless I go away, the Counselor will not come to you" (John 16).

The book of Acts, written by the same author as the gospel of Luke, tells what happened after Jesus' departure when the Counselor came at last. First, though, the disciples began adjusting to new realities: They selected a replacement for Judas, made plans to follow Jesus' final instructions, and returned to Jerusalem to await the Holy Spirit.

LIFE QUESTION: *Project yourself back to the forty-day period after Jesus' resurrection. What would you have been expecting Jesus to do?*

Explosion

KEY VERSE: Suddenly a sound like the blowing of a violent wind came from heaven and filled the whole house where they were sitting. . . . All of them were filled with the Holy Spirit and began to speak in other tongues as the Spirit enabled them. (Acts 2:2, 4)

On the feast day of Pentecost, the disciples got what they had been waiting for. Perhaps half a million pilgrims were milling about in Jerusalem on that Jewish holiday. The believers, in accord with Jesus' instructions, had gathered in a small group indoors, where they patiently awaited what had been promised. Then, with a sound like a violent wind and a sight like tongues of fire, it happened. The Holy Spirit, the Presence of God himself, took up residence inside ordinary bodies—their bodies.

The disciples hit the streets with a bold new style that the world has never recovered from. Soon everyone in Jerusalem was talking about the Jesus-followers. Clearly, something was afoot. To their amazement, pilgrims from all over the world heard the Galileans' message in their own native languages.

There was Peter, coward apostle who had denied Christ three times to save his own neck, brazenly taking on both Jewish and Roman authorities. Quoting from King David and the prophet Joel, he proclaimed that they had just lived through the most important event of all history. "God has raised this Jesus to life, and we are all witnesses of this fact," he said, and went on to declare Jesus as the very Messiah, the fulfillment of the Jews' long-awaited dream. Three thousand people responded to Peter's powerful message on that first day. And thus the Christian church was born.

Beginning with that boisterous scene in Jerusalem, Luke weaves a historical adventure tale. The group of new believers, at first a mere annoyance to the Jews and the Romans, would not stop growing. Just as Jesus had predicted, the message spread throughout Judea, and Samaria, and in less than one generation had penetrated into Rome, the center of civilization. In an era when new religions were a dime a dozen, the Christian faith became a worldwide phenomenon. It all began with this scene on the day of Pentecost.

LIFE QUESTION: *In this chapter, search for all the positive qualities that helped attract others to the new group of believers.*

Shock Waves

KEY VERSE:

Leave these men alone! Let them go! For if their purpose or activity is of human origin, it will fail. But if it is from God, you will not be able to stop these men; you will only find yourselves fighting against God. (Acts 5:38–39)

The disciples, newly empowered with the Holy Spirit, started acting a lot like Jesus. They went to the temple and preached sermons; they healed the sick; they met the needs of the poor. To many bystanders, the message of new life in Jesus sounded wonderful, like the first note of music to people born deaf. Five thousand men believed, including some priests. The followers were soon organizing and electing officers.

Acts also shows that problems sprang up alongside the successes. The church became popular, an "in" place to belong. Sorcerers and magicians dropped in, drawn by the reports of healings and other wonders. Wealthy people, like Ananias and Sapphira, saw the church as a place to gain applause for their benevolence. Such opportunists learned that the apostles, not to mention God, would not tolerate corruption in the fledgling church.

Before long, the focus of concern shifted away from internal problems to outside opposition. The same forces that had conspired against Jesus—temple officers, the Sadducees, the high priest, the Sanhedrin, Roman guards—aligned themselves against the new phenomenon of the church. Every so often they would haul in the leaders, but for what could they prosecute them—healing the sick? Inciting people to praise God? The Christians hardly resembled dangerous conspirators; they usually met openly on the temple porch.

Even so, religious leaders beat and jailed the apostles on trumped-up charges. What happened next should have given the establishment a clue into exactly what they were up against: The apostles responded to the beatings with praise to God for the privilege of suffering in his name, and an angel of the Lord sprang them free from jail.

Gamaliel, a wise old Pharisee, had perhaps the best advice of all (vv. 38–39). He could not have been more prophetic.

LIFE QUESTION: *What internal problems threaten the church today? What dangers come from outside?*

About-face

The most surprising converts often make the best crusaders. Former alcoholics can convince others of drinking's dangers; former drug addicts give the most forceful warnings against drugs. And when the book of Acts introduces the most effective Christian missionary of all time, he turns out to be a former bounty hunter of Christians.

KEY VERSE: *Barnabus took him and brought him to the apostles. He told them how Saul on his journey had seen the Lord and that the Lord had spoken to him, and how in Damascus he had preached fearlessly in the name of Jesus. (Acts 9:27)*

Acts 9 shows a glimpse of the early church even before it had a name; people called its followers "the Way," or "the brothers," or "the Nazarene sect." Its members lived in constant fear of arrest and persecution—if not from the Romans, then from the Jews. Already a leader named Stephen had been publicly stoned. And no one inspired more fear in the hearts of the early Christians than a man named Saul, who had participated in Stephen's execution.

But then came the miraculous turnabout on the road to Damascus. In a dramatic move, God stepped in and, against all odds, selected the bounty hunter Saul to lead the young church. It didn't take long to convince Saul: A blinding light and a voice from heaven knocked him out of commission for three days and changed his whole attitude toward Jesus. Such was Saul's murderous reputation, however, that the Christians in Damascus and Jerusalem accepted him only gradually.

Soon Saul (renamed Paul) was on the other end of the persecutors' whips; his former colleagues were now trying to kill *him*. He proved to be as fearless in preaching Christ as he had been in working against him. In four great missionary journeys, Paul took the news of the gospel around the shores of the Mediterranean. During those journeys he found time to write half the books of the New Testament, and in so doing laid the groundwork for Christian theology. Paul was perhaps the most thoroughly converted man who ever lived.

LIFE QUESTION: *Have you ever had an abrupt about-face?*

Moment of Crisis

KEY
VERSE:

Did you receive the Spirit by observing the law, or by believing what you heard? Are you so foolish? After beginning with the Spirit, are you now trying to attain your goal by human effort? (Gal.

All Jesus' disciples were Jewish, as were most of the converts from the day of Pentecost. But on his first missionary journey, Paul learned to his surprise that non-Jews were even more receptive to the news about Jesus. He began a policy that he would follow throughout his career: He went first to the synagogue and preached among Jews; if they rejected him, though, he turned immediately to the Gentiles.

In a twist of history, Paul gained a reputation as "the apostle to the Gentiles." Before conversion he had been a Pharisee, a strict Jewish legalist. But as he saw God work among non-Jews he became their champion. This letter to the churches in Galatia dates from the time of the early Jew-Gentile controversy. Paul is emotionally worked up. In fact, he is downright furious at misguided attempts to shackle the church with legalism. In the first paragraph, Paul explodes with full force; he then proceeds to give a "Christian," rather than Jewish, interpretation of the Old Testament covenants with Abraham and Moses.

Legalism may seem like a rather harmless quirk of the church, but Paul could foresee the outcome of the Galatians' thinking. They would start trusting in their own human effort (keeping "the Law") to gain acceptance with God. Faith in Christ would become just one of many steps in salvation, not the only one. The bedrock of the gospel would crumble as they, in effect, devalued what Christ had done.

Paul's letter to the Galatians is, then, a protest against treason. Paul insists that faith in Christ alone, not anyone's set of laws, opens the door to acceptance by God. If a person could reach God by obeying the Law, then he, the strict Pharisee, would have done it. Galatians teaches that there is nothing we can do to make God love us more, or love us less. We can't "earn" God's love by slavishly following rules.

LIFE QUESTION: *The Galatians got obsessed with legalism. Others refused to follow anyone's rules. Which seems the greater danger?*

Detour

The book of Acts follows Paul on three distinct missionary journeys. It was a good time in history to travel, for by Paul's lifetime Rome had established absolute mastery over a vast territory. Language was unified, and a rare empire-wide peace, the Pax Romana, prevailed. Moreover, Roman engineers had crisscrossed the empire with a network of roads (built so well that many still survive), and as a Roman citizen, Paul held a passport valid anywhere.

In his travels, Paul concentrated on the chief trade towns and capital cities of Roman colonies. From them, the gospel message could radiate out across the globe. If a young church showed promise, Paul would stay on, sometimes as long as three years, to direct its spiritual growth. His letters glow with affection for the friends he developed in this way. On his second and third journeys, Paul revisited many of the churches he had founded.

This chapter shows how one of Paul's favorite churches came into existence. Philippi was a leading city in the region of Macedonia, where a divine vision had directed him. Following his normal procedure, Paul had arranged his missionary trip strategically, linking together major towns and cities in sequence. But this one time he ran into a roadblock and received an alternative itinerary. A casual conversation with a woman by a river opened the way for Paul (women played a crucial role in many of the early churches). What took place in Philippi stands almost as a pattern for Paul's never-dull missionary visits: early acceptance, violent opposition, and providential deliverance from danger.

As this account reveals, Paul did not hesitate to use the prestige and status that came with his Roman citizenship. He was escorted from the city with proper respect, but he left behind two transformed households: one led by a woman cloth merchant, one, by a city jailer. From that unlikely combination would grow the lively church at Philippi.

LIFE QUESTION: *How have you sensed God's guidance in your life?*

Downward Mobility

KEY VERSE: *Do nothing out of selfish ambition or vain conceit, but in humility consider others better than yourselves. (Phil. 2:3)*

Fully a decade after founding the church, Paul wrote his Philippian friends a personal letter. He had suffered much in the intervening years: beatings, imprisonment, shipwreck, hostility from jealous competitors. Surely he must have sometimes wondered, "Is it worth all this pain?" Even as he wrote this letter, he was under arrest, "in chains for Christ" (1:13). But whenever Paul's thoughts turned to Philippi, the apostle's spirits lifted.

Paul declined gifts from most churches, out of fear that his enemies might twist the facts and accuse him of being a crook. But he trusted the Philippians. At least four separate times they sacrificed to meet his needs. Just recently, they had sent Epaphroditus on an arduous journey to care for Paul in prison. Paul wrote the book of Philippians, in fact, mainly as a thank-you for all that his friends had done.

If someone had bluntly asked the apostle, "Paul, tell me, what keeps you going through hard times?" he likely would have answered with words straight out of this chapter, for here Paul reveals the source of his irrepressible drive. First, Paul gives the example of Jesus. In a stately, hymnlike paragraph, he marvels that Jesus gave up all the glory of heaven to take on the form of a man—and not just a man, but a servant, one who poured out his life for others. Paul took on that pattern for himself.

Then, in a seeming paradox, Paul describes a kind of "teamwork" with God: While God is working within, we must "work out" salvation with fear and trembling. A later spiritual giant, Saint Teresa of Avila, expressed the paradox this way: "I pray as if all depends on God; I work as if all depends on me." Her formula aptly summarizes Paul's spiritual style.

Philippians gives an occasional glimpse of the apostle Paul's fatigue. But it also shows flashes of what kept him from "burnout." To him, the converts in Philippi shone "like stars in the universe." That kind of reward, and joy in their progress, kept Paul going.

LIFE QUESTION: *How can you "consider others better than yourself" without developing a bad self-image?*

Mixed Results

Jesus told a parable about a farmer sowing seed, some of which fell on rocky places, some among thorns, and some on fertile ground. This chapter, which reviews events from Paul's second journey, proves that he, the first foreign missionary, encountered all those responses in quick succession.

KEY VERSE: *A group of Epicurean and Stoic philosophers began to dispute with him. Some of them asked, "What is this babbler trying to say?" . . . They said this because Paul was preaching the good news about Jesus and the resurrection. (Acts 17:18)*

In Thessalonica, Paul's visit sparked a riot. An angry mob chased the apostle out of town, accusing him of causing "trouble all over the world." The next town, Berea, proved far more receptive. After studying the Scriptures to test out Paul's message, many believed, both Jews and non-Jews. Yet agitators from Thessalonica soon stirred up trouble there as well. (Paul was often trailed by hostile opponents who sought to confute his work.)

In Athens, Paul faced perhaps his most daunting missionary challenge. That renowned city of philosophers subjected each new thinker to a grueling intellectual ordeal. Local philosophers, full of scorn for Paul ("this babbler"), hauled him before the council of Areopagus that oversaw religion and morals.

Confident that the new faith could compete in the marketplace of ideas, Paul stood before the skeptical audience and, in a burst of eloquence, delivered the extraordinary speech contained in this chapter. Paul gained few converts among the elite Athenians, but he next traveled to the melting pot city of Corinth and founded a church remarkable for its ethnic diversity.

A modern-day evangelist assessing Paul's career said with a sigh, "Whenever the apostle Paul visited a city, the residents started a riot; when I visit one, they serve tea."

LIFE QUESTION: *What kind of approach to the gospel would work best in your community?*

Spiritual Checkup

Born in the midst of strife, the church at Thessalonica continued to meet hostility long after Paul was chased out of town. When he heard of their troubles, the apostle wrote this intimate letter, which provides important clues into what made him so effective as a "pastor." First Thessalonians, dating probably from A.D. 50 or 51, is our earliest record of the life of a Christian community. As such, it provides a firsthand account of Paul's relationship with a missionary church, barely twenty years after Jesus' departure.

KEY VERSE: *May the Lord make your love increase and overflow for each other and for everyone else, just as ours does for you. May he strengthen your hearts so that you will be blameless and holy. (1 Thess. 3:12–13)*

Paul reviews his pastoral style with the Thessalonians, reminding them that while among them, he was gentle and loving, "like a mother caring for her little children" (2:7). He writes as if he has only them on his mind all day long. He praises their strengths, fusses over their weaknesses, and continually thanks God for their spiritual progress. A recent report from Timothy has indicated they are heading down the right path, but Paul urges them to live for God and to love each other "more and more."

In this letter, Paul also answers criticisms that have been leveled against him. Is he in it for the money? Paul claims that during his sojourn with the Thessalonians he worked night and day (he supported himself as a tentmaker) to avoid becoming a financial burden. Has he abandoned them? Paul takes pains to explain the reasons behind his unavoidable absence.

Unlike some of Paul's other letters, 1 Thessalonians doesn't major in theology. Rather, it reveals the gratitude, disappointment, and joy of a beloved missionary who can't stop thinking about the church he left behind. Surely one reason for Paul's success centers on his churches having made as big an impression on Paul as he made on them.

LIFE QUESTION: *What seems to please Paul most about the Thessalonians? What worries him?*

Rumor Control

One topic dominates 2 Thessalonians more than any other: Jesus' return to earth. Church members were disturbed by a rumor, allegedly from Paul, that the last days had already arrived. In this letter, Paul denies the report and outlines what must occur before the day of the Lord arrives.

The controversy actually traces back to a portion of Paul's first letter. Toward the end of 1 Thessalonians, he gave direct answers to questions about the afterlife. Would people who had already died miss out on resurrection from the dead? It was more than an idle question for the Thessalonians, who lived with the constant danger of persecution. On any night a knock on the door could mean imprisonment or death.

Paul had allayed the Christians' fears by assuring them that people still living when Jesus returns to earth will rejoin those who have died before them. In the meantime, however, the Thessalonians had gone several steps beyond Paul's advice. Their speculation about the impending day of the Lord, fueled by the recent rumors, had become an obsession. Some of them had quit their jobs, and simply sat around in anticipation of that day. They were becoming, in Paul's words, "idle" and "busybodies."

Paul wrote 2 Thessalonians mainly to correct the imbalance. In the second chapter he tells of certain obscure events that must precede the second coming of Jesus. (No one is certain of Paul's exact meaning in every detail because he was building on teaching he had given the Thessalonians in private.)

Here, as elsewhere, the Bible does not focus on the last days in an abstract, theoretical way. Rather, it makes a practical application to how we should live. Paul counsels patience and steadiness. He asks his readers to trust that Jesus' return will finally bring justice to the earth, urges them to live worthily for that day, and commands them not to tolerate idleness—a good prescription for an obsession with the future in any time period.

LIFE QUESTION: *How should we prepare for Jesus' second coming?*

Out of the Melting Pot

Paul first visited the Grecian city of Corinth during one of the most stressful times of his career. Lynch mobs had chased him out of Thessalonica and Berea. The next stop, Athens, brought on confrontation with intellectual scoffers, and by the time Paul arrived at Corinth, he was in a fragile emotional state.

KEY VERSE: *Now the body is not made up of one part but of many. . . . You are the body of Christ, and each one of you is a part of it. (1 Cor. 12:14, 27)*

Shortly, opposition sprang up in Corinth. Jewish leaders hauled Paul into court. But in the midst of this crisis, God visited Paul with a special message of comfort: "I am with you, and no one is going to attack and harm you, because I have many people in this city" (Acts 18:10).

Those last words must have startled Paul, for Corinth was known mainly for its lewdness and drunken brawling. The Corinthians worshiped Venus, the goddess of love, and a temple built in her honor employed more than a thousand prostitutes. Thus Corinth seemed the last place on earth to expect a church to take root. Yet that's exactly what happened. A Jewish couple opened their home to Paul, and for the next eighteen months he stayed in Corinth to nurture an eager band of converts.

Corinth was filled with Orientals, Jews, Greeks, Egyptians, slaves, sailors, athletes, gamblers, and charioteers. And the Corinthian church reflected that same crazy-quilt pattern of diversity. When Paul wrote them this letter, he searched for a way to drive home the importance of Christian unity. He settled on a striking analogy from the human body. By comparing members of the church of Christ to individual parts of a human body, he could neatly illustrate how *diverse* members can work together in *unity*.

This analogy fit so well that it became Paul's favorite way of portraying the church. (He would refer to "the body of Christ" more than thirty times in his various letters.) Having also raised the question of how diverse people can work together in a spiritual body, he answered that question with a lyrical description of love, the greatest of all spiritual gifts.

LIFE QUESTION: *First Corinthians 13 describes ideal love. Which of these characteristics do you need to work on?*

The Last Enemy

Some people in Paul's day were challenging the Christian belief in an afterlife. Death, they said, is the end. Throughout history, many people have taken such a position. In Jesus' day, a Jewish sect called Sadducees denied the resurrection from the dead. Doubters persist today; among them are Black Muslims, Buddhists, Marxists, and most atheists. Some New Age advocates present death as a natural part of the cycle of life. Why consider it bad at all?

The Corinthian church soon learned not to voice such an attitude around the apostle Paul. Belief in an afterlife to him was no fairy tale; it was the fulcrum of his entire faith. If there's no future life, he thundered, the Christian message would be a lie. He, Paul, would have no reason to continue as a minister; Christ's death would have merely wasted blood; and Christians would be the most pitiable of all people on earth.

The Bible presents a gradually developing emphasis on the afterlife. Old Testament Jews had only the vaguest conception of life after death. But as Paul points out, Jesus' resurrection from the dead changed all that. Suddenly the world had primary proof that God had the power and the will to overcome death. Chapter 15 brings together the threads of Christian belief about death. With no hesitation, Paul brands death "the enemy," the last enemy to be destroyed.

This chapter often gets read at funerals, and with good reason. As people gather around a casket, they sense as if by instinct the *unnaturalness,* the horror, of death. To such people, to all of us, this passage offers soaring words of hope. Death is not an end, but a beginning.

LIFE QUESTION: *How does a belief in the afterlife affect your life now?*

Hope During Hard Times

Paul blasted anyone who, as the phrase goes, "is too heavenly-minded to be of any earthly good." He did *not* prepare for the next life by sitting around all day waiting for it to happen. Paul worked as hard as anyone has ever worked, but with a new purpose: "We make it our goal to please him, whether we are at home in the body or away from it." He sought to do God's will on earth just as it is done in heaven.

This passage shows that Paul's hope for the future kept him motivated when the crush of life tempted him to "lose heart." He wrote this letter just as an intense struggle with the Corinthian church was coming to a head, and as a result it reveals the apostle in one of his lowest, most vulnerable moments. He describes his present state as "hard pressed on every side, but not crushed; perplexed, but not in despair; persecuted, but not abandoned; struck down, but not destroyed."

In typical style, Paul uses a word picture to express his inner thoughts: "treasure in jars of clay." In his day, jars of clay were nearly as common, and as disposable, as cardboard boxes are today. Beset by difficulties, Paul felt as durable as one of those fragile jars. Yet he recognized that God had chosen to entrust the gospel, and its good news of forgiveness and eternal life, to such ordinary people as himself.

That insight seemed to give Paul renewed hope. He offers a stirring example of how a future life with God can affect a person on earth: "Therefore we do not lose heart. Though outwardly we are wasting away, yet inwardly we are being renewed day by day. For our light and momentary troubles are achieving for us an eternal glory that far outweighs them all. So we fix our eyes not on what is seen, but on what is unseen. For what is seen is temporary, but what is unseen is eternal."

LIFE QUESTION: *What kind of person would Paul call a success? A failure?*

Paul Answers His Critics

KEY VERSE: *For Christ's sake, I delight in weaknesses, in insults, in hardships, in persecutions, in difficulties. For when I am weak, then I am strong.*

Jewish and Roman establishments viewed Paul as a major threat, but he had expected their opposition. What bothered him far more was antagonism from fellow Christians. Jealous competitors had infiltrated the Corinthian church, spreading rumors to undercut Paul's reputation. He wasn't fully Jewish, they charged. He didn't deserve the title "apostle" since he had not followed Jesus on earth. And, like other false teachers, he was in it for the money.

In his letters to the Corinthians Paul confesses a reluctance to defend himself—"I am out of my mind to talk like this"—but their criticisms had gotten out of hand. Jewish? Paul was a strict Pharisee who had studied with the famous teacher Gamaliel. Apostle? True, Paul had not served as one of the twelve disciples. But he had met the risen Jesus on the road to Damascus, and was later granted a special revelation of "inexpressible things, things that man is not permitted to tell." Exploiter? Paul had supported himself financially to avoid taking money from the church.

Paul then begins to "boast" about his weaknesses. He runs through the amazing list of beatings, imprisonments, insults, and hardships that have marked his career. And he balances off his veiled reference to the special vision with a frank account of one urgent prayer that has never been answered.

Three times Paul had asked God to remove a mysterious "thorn in the flesh." Bible scholars don't agree on the precise nature of the "thorn." Some suggest a physical ailment, such as an eye disease, malaria, or epilepsy. Others interpret it as a spiritual temptation, or a series of failures in his ministry. Whatever the ailment, Paul stresses that God declined to remove the thorn, despite all his prayers for relief, in order to teach him an important lesson about humility, grace, and dependence.

Paul never seemed to get over the wonder of the fact that God had chosen him, a former enemy, to bear the good news. He felt humbled and honored that even his weaknesses, *especially* his weaknesses, could be used to advance the kingdom.

LIFE QUESTION: *How has God spoken to you through your "weaknesses"?*

Paul's
Legacy

Where All Roads Led

Throughout his arduous and adventurous life, the apostle Paul kept one career goal constantly before him: a visit to Rome. In his day, Rome was the center of everything—law, culture, power, and learning. From that capital, a powerful empire ruled over the entire Western world.

A tiny new church had formed there, causing great excitement among other Christians. They knew that in some ways the future of the worldwide church rested on what happened in Rome. If they ever expected to make a dent in the larger world, they would have to penetrate Rome.

Paul prayed for the Roman church constantly and made many plans to visit there. He wrote this letter in preparation for his long-awaited visit.

Unlike the letters to the Corinthians, Romans contains few personal asides or emotional outbursts. Paul was addressing sophisticated, demanding readers, most of whom he had never met. In the letter he sought to set forth the whole scope of Christian doctrine, which was still being passed along orally from town to town. The resulting book has no equal as a concise, yet all-encompassing summation of the Christian faith.

Romans is a book to savor slowly and carefully. The logic of Paul's argument unfolds thought by thought from the first chapter. He is presenting the good news about God's amazing grace: A complete cure is available to all. But people won't seek a cure until they know they are ill. Thus Romans begins with, and this passage adjoins, one of the darkest summaries in the Bible. "There is no one righteous, not even one," Paul concludes. The entire world is doomed to spiritual death unless a cure can be found.

Out of the mournful notes, however, comes a bright sound of wonderful news, expressed in what some have called the central theological passage in the Bible. Paul expresses the core message of the gospel in a mere eleven verses (3:21–31).

LIFE QUESTION: *Paul uses mostly legal terminology in verses 21–31. How would you express the same truths in your own words?*

Limits of the Law

By dying to what once bound us, we have been released from the law so that we serve in the new way of the Spirit, and not in the old way of the written code. (Rom. 7:6)

*O*ne issue comes up in virtually every one of Paul's letters: "What good is the law?" To most of Paul's readers, the word *law* stood for the huge collection of rules and rituals codified from the Old Testament. Thanks to his earlier days as a Pharisee, Paul knew those rules well. And whenever he started talking about "the new covenant," or "freedom in Christ," the Jews wanted to know what he now thought about that law.

This chapter, the most personal and autobiographical in Romans, discloses exactly what Paul thought.

Paul never recommended throwing out the Law entirely. He saw that it reveals a basic code of morality, an ideal of the kind of behavior that pleases God. The Law is good for one thing: It exposes sin. "Indeed I would not have known what sin was except through the Law." To Paul, such rules as The Ten Commandments were helpful, righteous, and good.

There is one problem with the Law, however: Although it proves how bad you are, it doesn't make you any better. During his days of legalism, Paul had developed a very sensitive conscience, but, as he poignantly recounts, it mainly made him feel guilty all the time. "What a wretched man I am!" he confessed. The Law bared his weaknesses but could not provide the power needed to overcome them. The Law—or *any* set of rules—leads ultimately to a dead end.

Romans 7 gives a striking illustration of the struggle that ensues when an imperfect person commits himself to a perfect God. Any Christian who wonders "How can I ever get rid of my nagging sins?" will find comfort in Paul's frank confession. In the face of God's standards, every one of us feels helpless, and that is Paul's point precisely. No set of rules can break the terrible cycle of guilt and failure. We need outside help to "serve in the new way of the Spirit, and not in the old way of the written code." Paul celebrates that help in the next chapter.

LIFE QUESTION: *What personal struggle makes you feel most "helpless"? Where do you turn?*

Spirit Life

KEY VERSE: *There is now no condemnation for those who are in Christ Jesus, because through Christ Jesus the law of the Spirit of life set me free from the law of sin and death. (Rom. 8:1–2)*

The Holy Spirit is the theme of Romans 8, and in it Paul gives a panoramic survey of how the Spirit can make a difference in a person's life.

First, Paul sets to rest the nagging problem of sin he has just raised so forcefully. "There is now no condemnation. . . ." he announces. Jesus Christ, through his life and death, took care of "the sin problem" for all time.

Elsewhere (Romans 4), Paul borrows a word from banking to explain the process. God "credits" Jesus' own perfection to our accounts, so that we are judged not by our behavior, but by his. Similarly, God has transferred all the punishment we deserve onto Jesus, through his death on the cross. In this transaction, human beings come out the clear winners, set free at last from the curse of sin.

And, as always with Paul, the best news of all is that Jesus Christ did not stay dead. Paul marvels that the very same power that raised Christ from the dead can also "enliven" us. The Spirit is a life-giver who alone can break the gloomy, deathlike pattern described in Romans 7.

To be sure, the Spirit does not remove all problems. His very titles—Intercessor, Helper, Counselor, Comforter—assume there will be problems. But the God within is able to do for us what we could never do for ourselves. The Spirit works alongside us as we relate to God, helping us in our weakness, even praying for us when we don't know what to ask.

The way Paul tells it, what happens inside individual believers is the central drama of history: "All of creation waits in eager expectation for the sons of God to be revealed." Somehow, spiritual victories within us will help bring about the liberation and healing of a "groaning" creation. The apostle can hardly contain himself as he contemplates these matters. Romans 8 ends with a ringing declaration that nothing—*absolutely, positively nothing*—can ever separate us from God's love. For Paul, that was a fact worth shouting about.

LIFE QUESTION: *According to this chapter, how can the Holy Spirit make a difference in your daily life?*

Getting Down to Earth

Too often theology is viewed as stuff for hermits to think about. When there's nothing else to do, *then* is the time to ask abstract questions about God. Such a notion would have exasperated the apostle Paul. To him, theology was worthless unless it made a difference in how people lived. Thus, after laying out the most thorough, concise summary of Christian theology in the Bible, he turns his attention at the end of Romans to a down-to-earth discussion of everyday problems.

Paul's own life offers a good example of how to make theology practical. In fact, he wrote the lofty book of Romans while traveling to raise funds for famine relief. By collecting offerings from gentile Christians for the sake of Jews in Jerusalem, Paul modeled the kind of unity sorely needed by both groups. (See 2 Corinthians 8 for more details of this mercy mission.)

Romans 12 needs no special commentary or study aids. The problem lies not in understanding these words, but in obeying them. Paul is describing what love in action should look like. Once more he uses the analogy of the human body to illustrate how diverse parts can work together in unity.

"Offer your bodies as living sacrifices," Paul urged his readers. The Romans, both Jews and Gentiles, associated the word "sacrifices" with the lambs and other animals they brought to the temple for priests to kill on an altar. But Paul makes clear that God wants *living* human beings, not dead animals. A person committed to God's will is the kind of offering most pleasing to God.

LIFE QUESTION: *Use verses 9–21 as a kind of checklist. Which commands do you have the most trouble with? Which are the easiest?*

Unexpected Passage

*F*riends begged Paul not to go to Jerusalem, still a hotbed of persecution against the Christians. But Paul, "compelled by the Spirit" (20:22), persisted. He knew that God wanted him to carry his word to Rome, and no disaster in Jerusalem could interfere with that plan.

When Paul reached Jerusalem, the worst happened: He was arrested on trumped-up charges. Forty Jewish fanatics vowed not to eat or drink until they had killed Paul. His reputation as a Christian missionary had so aroused the conspirators that it took a brigade of 470 Roman soldiers to protect him.

The last few chapters of Acts show Pault his most fearless. He boldly confronted a lynch mob until Roman soldiers had to drag him into barracks for his own protection. The next day, he took on the Jewish ruling body, the Sanhedrin, causing such a ruckus that the Roman commander feared they would tear Paul in pieces. In the midst of all this turmoil, Paul got a comforting vision from the Lord, who said, "Take courage! As you have testified about me in Jerusalem, so you must also testify in Rome" (23:11).

After being smuggled out of town under heavy guard and the cover of darkness, Paul arrived at last in the palace of the Roman governor. His troubles were far from over. After hearing Paul's defense, Felix sent him to prison for two years, as a political favor to the Jews. Even that did not quiet the furor. The moment the new governor Festus arrived, Jewish leaders hatched yet another death plot against Paul.

Acts preserves three of the speeches delivered by Paul on trial. Roman officials would bring him out to perform, like a circus sideshow. As always, Paul made the best of his opportunities. This chapter records the impression he made on the most distinguished judge of all, King Herod Agrippa.

As a result of the Romans' inquisitions, Paul got his long-awaited trip to Rome—not via a missionary journey, but in a Roman ship as a prisoner of the empire.

LIFE QUESTION: *If you were prosecuted for your beliefs, what might be said in your defense speech?*

Prisoner in Charge

*A*fter surviving assassination plots, riots, imprisonment, and a corrupt judicial system, Paul encountered a new set of obstacles on his voyage to Rome. This chapter gives an eyewitness account of an ocean storm, the once-in-a-decade kind of storm that survivors would never forget. Dense clouds blotted out the sun and stars for many days; the entire shipload of 276 passengers and crew went without food for two weeks, and no one knew whether they would survive to see another day. No one, that is, except the apostle Paul.

Luke, a passenger accompanying Paul (note the prominent word "we"), recounts the experience in vivid detail. He depicts the frenzy onboard: sailors lashing ropes around their groaning ship, the crew heaving precious food supplies and even the ship's tackle overboard, Roman soldiers with drawn swords halting the sailors' save-our-own-necks escape attempts and preparing to slash their prisoners' throats. In the midst of all this hysteria stands the apostle Paul, perfectly calm, foretelling what will happen next. God had promised the apostle would visit Rome, a vision confirmed it, and Paul never doubted, even when the boat broke in pieces around him.

Once more, Paul reveals himself as a man of unassailable courage. The Roman centurion surely recognized it: He granted Paul extraordinary privileges and protection. By the end of the storm, everyone on the ship was following the advice of the strange, unflappable prisoner from Tarsus.

LIFE QUESTION: *How do you normally react in a crisis?*

Rome at Last

Boldly and without hindrance he preached the kingdom of God and taught about the Lord Jesus Christ. (Acts 28:31)

The future of the gentile church depended in large measure on what happened to Paul. Thus the last few chapters of Acts portray a kind of spiritual warfare in which God turns apparent tragedy into good. Paul gets arrested; he's sent at last to Rome. The ship wrecks; they all survive. A poisonous snake bites Paul; he shakes it off and starts a healing ministry.

Paul arrived in Rome, his ultimate destination, under guard. Undoubtedly the reputation he had gained on the voyage helped convince authorities to treat him leniently. He lived by himself under a kind of "house arrest." A soldier was always present, possibly chained to the apostle. In typical fashion, Paul put his time to good use. The very first week he called in Jewish leaders to explain to them the Christian "sect" everyone was talking about. Over the next months and years Paul got hours of quiet solitude to work on fond letters to the churches he had left behind.

Luke details the process of Roman justice so thoroughly that some have speculated he wrote Acts as a legal brief for Paul's defense. Was Paul intent on inciting revolt? Luke meticulously records that Paul had no political ambitions and consistently worked within Roman law.

Luke breaks off the story with Paul's fate still undecided. Most scholars believe that Paul, released from this imprisonment, went on to take his message to new frontiers. Luke records nothing of those journeys, and nothing about Paul's trial or sentencing. He ends with a single memory, frozen in time: Paul, confined to his house, preaching to all his visitors. Paul could no longer choose his audience; they had to seek him. But boldly, in the heart of mighty Rome, he proclaimed a new kingdom and a new king. Christianity had made the journey, and the transition, from Jerusalem to Rome.

Tradition records that a few years later the Emperor Nero had Paul executed. The final verse of Acts serves as a fitting epitaph of the apostle's remarkable career.

LIFE QUESTION: *Do you, like Paul, strive to "make the best" of bad situations?*

Looking Up

*Ironically, some of the brightest, most hopeful books of the Bible—the letters to the Philippians, Colossians, and Ephesians—came out of Paul's term of house arrest in Rome. There's a good reason: Prison offered him the precious commodity of time. Paul was no longer journeying from town to town, stamping out fires set by his enemies. Settled into passably comfortable surroundings, he could devote attention to lofty thoughts about the meaning of life.

KEY VERSE:

I pray also that the eyes of your heart may be enlightened in order that you may know the hope to which he has called you, the riches of his glorious inheritance in the saints, and his incomparably great power for us who believe. (Eph. 1:18–19)

A prisoner who survived fourteen years in a Cuban jail told how he kept his spirits up: "The worst part was the monotony. I had no window in my cell, and so I mentally constructed one on the door. I 'saw' in my mind a beautiful scene from the mountains, with water tumbling down a ravine over rocks. It became so real to me that I would visualize it without effort every time I looked at the cell door."

The letter to Ephesians gives a hint as to what the apostle Paul "saw" when he let his mind wander beyond the monotony of his place of confinement. First, he visualized the spiritual growth in the churches he had left behind. This passage opens with a burst of thanksgiving for the vitality of the Ephesian church. Then, he sought to open "the eyes of their hearts" to even more exalted sights: the "incomparable riches" of God's grace.

Ephesians is full of staggering good news. In it, Paul asks the grandest question of all: "What is God's overall purpose for this world?" He raises the sights far above his own circumstances to bigger issues, cosmic issues. And when he cranks up the volume to express God's plan of love, not one low, mournful note sneaks in.

If you feel discouraged, or wonder if God really cares, or question whether the Christian life is worth the effort, Ephesians provides a great tonic. It prescribes the "riches in Christ" available to all.

LIFE QUESTION: *What do you find most encouraging about Paul's good-news message?*

A Checkered Past

KEY VERSE:
His purpose was to create in himself one new man out of the two, thus making peace, and in this one body to reconcile both of them to God through the cross, by which he put to death their hostility. (Eph. 2:15–16)

The missionary church at Ephesus was one of Paul's success stories. It was renowned for religion—but not the kind of religion Paul represented. Worship of the Roman goddess Diana centered in Ephesus, and its residents took great pride in the temple devoted to her. The temple building ranked among the seven wonders of the ancient world, and inside it hundreds of professional prostitute-priestesses assisted the "worshipers."

In that unlikely place, Paul discovered a tiny Christian community already in existence. They knew something about John the Baptist, not much about Jesus, and had never even heard of the Holy Spirit. For the next two years Paul preached to the Jews and to the Gentiles. A burgeoning church took root, and soon word spread throughout the entire province of Asia. Ephesian merchants, who made their living on profitable sales of idols, finally chased Paul out of town. (See Acts 19 for background.)

Like most early churches, the one at Ephesus struggled with Jew-Gentile differences. Believers from a Jewish background, raised on a steady diet of anti-idolatry, had huge obstacles to overcome in accepting former idol-worshipers into their church. This section of Ephesians addresses the unity issues head-on.

In keeping with the spirit of this letter, and the healthy state of the church, Paul maintains an upbeat tone. He presents Christ as the great destroyer of barriers, the one who demolishes walls of division. (The Jewish temple in Jerusalem had an actual wall that no Gentile could go beyond.)

To Paul, the new community in Ephesus formed of both Jews and Gentiles was one of the great mysteries of the ages, a culmination of God's original plan, kept secret for many centuries, but now made known. Paul can hardly contain his soaring spirit, and language, as he marvels at God's plan being fulfilled at that moment.

LIFE QUESTION: *In Paul's time, Jews and Gentiles were two groups given to quarreling and division. What groups divide churches today?*

205

Christ is Enough

KEY VERSE: *. . . So that they may have the full riches of complete understanding, in order that they may know the mystery of God, namely, Christ, in whom are hidden all the treasures of wisdom and knowledge. (Col. 2:2–3)*

The book of Colossians may sound like Ephesians, and with good reason—fully half the verses in Ephesians appear in some form in Colossians. The two cities were neighbors, and one of the converts from Paul's stay in Ephesus had taken the gospel over to Colosse. Paul himself had never visited Colosse, and thus wrote this book to people who knew him by reputation only.

The letter opens on an optimistic note, with Paul thanking God for the Colossians' spiritual progress. Yet he also brings up for discussion a doctrinal flaw that had crept into their church. The best modern equivalent would be a "cult," one that includes some Christian principles overlaid with many other mysterious beliefs.

First-century Colosse, situated on a major trade route from the East, was a perfect breeding ground for cults. Even Jews in that area worshiped angels and river spirits. Often these cults (like many now) did not reject Jesus Christ outright; they merely worked him into a more elaborate scheme. Christ and simple forms of worship, they taught, were fine for beginners; however, for the "deep things of God," some further steps were required. Rather than attacking each peculiar belief point by point, Paul counters with a positive theology. "Christ is enough," he declares in this first chapter. He is God, the fullness of God, the one who made the world, the reason that everything exists. All the "mystery" and treasure and wisdom you could ask for are found in the person of Jesus Christ. There is no need to look elsewhere. The masterful summation paragraph that begins at verse 15 may have been adapted for use as a hymn by the early church.

Paul tells the Colossians just what he had told the Ephesians: Before Christ, a mystery was kept hidden for many centuries. But when Christ came, everything broke out into the open. The fullness of God lived, died, and then reappeared after death—all in broad daylight. Why settle for counterfeits?

LIFE QUESTION: *Who is trying to deceive people by "fine-sounding arguments" today?*

A Personal Favor

KEY VERSE: *I appeal to you for my son Onesimus, who became my son while I was in chains. (Philem. v.10)*

The New Testament includes four of the apostle Paul's letters to individuals (Philemon, Titus, 1 and 2 Timothy). Of these, Philemon is the briefest, and also the most personal. Paul is writing a friend to ask a favor—a *big* favor, for a person's life hangs in the balance.

Like most respectable citizens of his day, Philemon owned slaves. One of these, Onesimus, had stolen from his master and run away to Rome. There, he met Paul and became a Christian.

As a Christian, the slave Onesimus felt the need to make restitution to his master, whom he had wronged. But the laws of the empire were merciless to runaway slaves. If Onesimus returned, his master Philemon had the legal power to sentence him to immediate execution. Or, he could brand the letter *F* (for *Fugitivus*) on his forehead with a hot iron, marking him for life.

The apostle Paul agreed to use his full influence on Philemon, and this brief letter, a masterpiece of persuasion and diplomacy, is the result. Paul appeals to Philemon's friendship, his status as a Christian leader, his sense of love and compassion. He applies blatant pressure, reminding Philemon that "you owe me your very self." He even offers to pay back Onesimus's debts.

Paul does not call for the outright abolition of slavery in this letter. Such a call would have threatened the economic base of the empire and brought the crushing weight of Rome down on the fledgling church. In fact, slavery would endure for another 1,800 years after this letter was written. The tiny book of Philemon, however, shows that faith had a profound impact on slavery long before its abolition.

Onesimus, his Christian conscience pricked, was assuming a grave risk by turning himself in. In Philemon, Paul asks for a second act of faith, by pleading with the slave's owner to "welcome him as you would welcome me." Onesimus was no longer "property," but rather a Christian brother. Such an attitude in that culture was social dynamite.

LIFE QUESTION: *Do you know of any situations in which you could be a reconciler?*

Paul's Trouble-shooter

KEY VERSE: *Set them an example by doing what is good. In your teaching show integrity, seriousness and soundness of speech that cannot be condemned, so that those who oppose you may be ashamed because they have nothing bad to say about us. (Titus 2:7–8)*

In his early years, Paul, in a whirlwind of energy, had personally carried the message of the gospel to the far corners of the Near East. But age and poor health gradually slowed him down, and he spent many of his later years locked away in prison. Increasingly, he turned to loyal helpers to carry on his work.

The name Titus appears fourteen times in Paul's letters. The book of Galatians (2:1–5) introduces him as Paul's "exhibit A" proving that a Gentile could become a fully acceptable Christian. For more than a decade Paul relied on his trusted associate, who seemed to specialize in crisis churches. Twice Titus was dispatched on a diplomatic mission to the rowdy church at Corinth. This letter indicates he faced an equally challenging task on Crete. Paul was writing him a set of personal instructions on how to handle a difficult assignment.

Crete, an island in the Mediterranean, had an ethnically divided population. Its main knowledge of the outside world came through pirates and coarse sailors. You can get an idea of the challenges Titus faced there by reading between the lines of Paul's advice. For example, Paul's advice to the older men to "be temperate, worthy of respect, self-controlled" reveals something about their normal patterns; likewise, his charge to the women "not to be slanderers or addicted to much wine." One of the island's own poets had described Cretans as "liars, evil brutes, lazy gluttons."

Paul always kept in mind that the Christian church, as a new phenomenon, would attract close scrutiny from the outside world. In Titus, he gives advice on how each of the diverse groups in the church—older men, older women, younger women, young men, slaves—could provide the best example for that watching world. The goal: "so that those who oppose you may be ashamed because they have nothing bad to say about us."

LIFE QUESTION: *Of the advice Paul gives to the various groups, which applies most directly to you?*

Growing Pains

KEY VERSE: *I give you this instruction in keeping with the prophecies once made about you, so that by following them you may fight the good fight. (1 Tim. 1:18)*

The role of women in the church, a Christian's relationship to society, fund-rasing techniques, social welfare programs, materialism, order of worship—the list could describe the agenda for a modern-day denominational convention. But the apostle Paul was already addressing these issues in the first century, just a few decades after Jesus' life on earth.

Actually, the problems discussed in 1 Timothy represent growing pains. For example, out of Christian compassion Christians had extended help to needy widows. But before long, some members with a "welfare mentality" saw the widows' list as an easy way to avoid financial responsibility for their families. In 1 Timothy, Paul outlines a form of "enrollment" to establish who was truly needy.

These and other problems were afflicting the church at Ephesus where Timothy now served as pastor. The church had grown and thrived despite intense opposition from within that secular city. The letter to the Ephesians was one of Paul's happiest, but now, almost ten years after his visit to Ephesus, Paul has learned of major troubles brewing. The time had come for older churches to get organized and to bring some order to their worship and outreach programs. Otherwise, they would drift toward endless division and disagreement.

For that thankless job, Paul turned to his trusted companion Timothy. Given his shyness and his half-Jewish/half-Gentile ancestry, Timothy did not seem the ideal choice for a heresy fighter in a turbulent church. But Paul was convinced he could do the job. "I have no one else like him," Paul once wrote of Timothy. "As a son with his father he has served with me in the work of the gospel" (Philippians 2). Through disturbances, riots, and even into prison, Timothy had loyally accompanied the apostle. Despite a weak stomach and timid disposition, Timothy had proved his mettle to Paul in many ways, and Paul wrote this letter to encourage him in a difficult task.

LIFE QUESTION: *Do you have any personality traits that make Christian service seem difficult?*

Final Words

I am suffering even to the point of being chained like a criminal. But God's word is not chained." Those words from Paul to Timothy sum up both his personal plight and his burning desire to see his life's work continue after his death.

The second letter to Timothy contains many clues about Paul's circumstances. He is imprisoned in Rome once again, but this time the treatment seems far harsher than the previous house arrest. Now he is being kept in chains, in a cold dungeon that his friends can barely locate. Paul's spirits are sagging. He feels abandoned by "everyone in the province of Asia" (1:15).

This letter almost certainly dates from the time of Emperor Nero, around A.D. 66–67. By then Christianity had grown from a splinter sect of Judaism into a major force with many thousands of converts, and Nero seized upon it as a scapegoat for the ills of the empire. Soon the crazed emperor was torturing believers by crucifying them, by wrapping them in animal skins and turning his hunting dogs loose on them, and by burning them alive as human torches to illuminate the games in his garden.

Little wonder that Paul, imprisoned in that era, exhorted Timothy on the need for boldness in the face of suffering. Paul's own life was nearing an end, and he wrote these, his last recorded words, as a legacy to pass on to Timothy and other "reliable men who will also be qualified to teach others."

Second Timothy is a moody book. Sometimes Paul makes himself vulnerable, exposing his fears and his loneliness. Other times, as in this chapter, he gives a rousing "pep talk" meant to cheer Timothy's spirits—and perhaps his own. Life was closing in on the apostle, and he strings together last-minute reminders: advice on pure living, essential nuggets of theology, inspiring analogies, one-line proverbs, warnings, common sayings. There is no particular order to this book; Paul has no time for that. He is setting down a kind of spiritual "last will and testament" for his son in Christ.

LIFE QUESTION: *What issues seem to concern Paul most as he faces death?*

Vital
Letters

Why Better?

Are religions all that different?" skeptics ask. "Isn't the most important thing to be sincere in whatever you believe?" Such "modern" questions have, in fact, been debated for thousands of years. The book of Hebrews was written in response to people torn between the Jewish religion and the new faith of Christianity.

Some favored sticking with the familiar routine of Judaism, which had centuries-old traditions behind it. Another advantage: The Jews enjoyed Rome's official protection, while Christians were subject to persecution. Was faith in Christ worth the risk?

Hebrews insists there are decisive reasons to choose Christ. The whole book is constructed around the word *better*. Jesus is better than the angels, or Moses, or the Old Testament way—better than anything the world has to offer.

Yet, after recording a gust of grand theology from the Psalms, the author of Hebrews seems to pause and reconsider, "At present we do not see everything subject to him." Could a world in which Christians were being arrested, tortured, and tossed into jail really be subject to Christ?

From there, the author explains why it mattered that God descended to the world and became a human being. He did not magically remove all human problems, but rather *subjected himself* to the same hardships that any of us face. Hebrews goes further than any other New Testament book in explaining Jesus' human nature.

This chapter gives two powerful reasons why Jesus came to earth. First, by dying, he freed us from the power of death and won for us eternal life. And second, by experiencing normal human temptations, he can better help us with our own temptations.

No angel, and no God in distant heaven, could have accomplished those things. Jesus came, in effect, on a rescue mission, to free humanity from slavery. Apart from Christ, we live in constant fear of death and in constant bondage to our failures, or sins. Only Jesus can set us free. That's why he's worth the risk.

LIFE QUESTION: *According to this chapter, what "advantages" does Jesus offer you?*

Tough Faith

KEY VERSE: *Now faith is being sure of what we hope for and certain of what we do not see. This is what the ancients were commended for. (Heb. 11:1–2)*

The last few paragraphs of chapter 10 reveal much about the original readers of Hebrews. Converting to Christ had brought them much abuse: confiscation of property, public insult, and even imprisonment. In the early days, they accepted such persecution gladly, even joyfully. But as time went on, and the trials continued, some were beginning to lose heart.

To these discouraged people, Hebrews 11 presents a stirring reminder of what constitutes "true faith." It's tempting to think of faith as a kind of magic formula: If you muster up enough of it, you'll get rich, stay healthy, and live a contented life with automatic answers to all your prayers. But the readers of Hebrews were discovering that life does not work according to such neat formulas. As proof, the author painstakingly reviews the lives of some Old Testament giants of faith. (Some have dubbed Hebrews 11 the "Faith Hall of Fame.")

"Without faith," Hebrews says bluntly, "it is impossible to please God." But the author uses rather pointed words in describing that faith: "persevere," "endure," "don't lose heart." As a result of their faith, some heroes triumphed: They routed armies, escaped the sword, survived lions. But many others met less happy ends: They were flogged, chained, stoned, sawed in two. The chapter concludes, "These were all commended for their faith, yet none of them received what had been promised."

The picture of faith that emerges from this chapter does not fit into an easy formula. Sometimes faith leads to victory and triumph. Sometimes it requires a gritty determination to "hang on at any cost." Hebrews 11 does not hold up one kind of faith as superior to the other. Both rest on the belief that God is in ultimate control and will indeed keep his promises, whether in this life or in the next. Of such people, Hebrews says, "God is not ashamed to be called their God, for he has prepared a city for them."

LIFE QUESTION: *In your own life of faith do you identify with the victorious heroes of faith or with those who "hang on at any cost"?*

Marathon Race

KEY
VERSE:

Let us throw off everything that hinders and the sin that so easily entangles, and let us run with perseverance the race marked out for us. (Heb. 12:1)

Hebrews 12 takes up right where the previous chapter left off, only the author moves the spotlight from Old Testament history to the readers themselves. He likens faith to an athletic contest in a stadium. Those who have gone before—the giants of faith from chapter 11—are like "a great cloud of witnesses" watching the rest of us run the race of faith. Therefore, "throw off everything that hinders," Hebrews coaches, and again, "strengthen your feeble arms and weak knees."

Evidently, the original readers of Hebrews had expected a short sprint, not a grueling marathon run. They needed encouragement and discipline to survive a long-distance spiritual contest.

The analogy of a marathon race provides a convenient way to think about the Christian life. Why do people punish their bodies through a twenty-six-mile course? Most runners mention a sense of personal accomplishment, combined with the physical benefits of exercise. There are parallel benefits in a "spiritual marathon." Applying the discipline needed to resist temptation, and to endure hardship, leads to certain good results: namely, strong character and a clean conscience. Not to mention the eternal rewards that await all who finish the race.

True competitors set their sights on the lead runner, and as might be expected, Hebrews holds up Jesus as the ultimate standard for our faith. He endured the terrible suffering of the cross for the sake of "the joy set before him." Because of Jesus, no one can complain, "God doesn't know what it's like down here." He does know, for he, too, has been here. And for anyone tempted to grow weary and lose heart, the very best cure is to "fix your eyes on Jesus, the author and perfecter of our faith."

The chapter ends with a soaring passage that celebrates how much better is Christ's new covenant than the old one between God and the Israelites. The new covenant will culminate in a new creation and a new kingdom—one that can never be shaken.

LIFE QUESTION: *If maturing spiritually is like a marathon race, how far along are you?*

Practice
What You Preach

You get a sense of James's style in the first two sentences of his letter. After the sparsest of greetings, he dives directly into the topic at hand and starts dishing out advice. James lacked the education and sophistication of the apostle Paul, so you won't find his letter wandering off into abstract theology. He was a simple man, a man of the soil. He drew analogies from nature—ocean waves, wilted flowers, a forest fire, spring rains—and expressed his thoughts in pithy sayings almost like proverbs.

Since James's church in Jerusalem was one of the main targets of Jewish persecution, it's natural that his letter begins with encouragement for people undergoing trials. But it quickly moves on to a variety of topics, in each case exhorting readers to live out their beliefs. *Be humble!* James orders. *Control your tongue! Stop sinning!* James is as forthright as an Old Testament prophet. It's hard to miss his point.

One verse in the first chapter neatly summarizes the pervasive message of this book: "Do not merely listen to the word, and so deceive yourselves. Do what it says." James offers up a very pointed illustration of exactly the kind of hypocrisy he is talking about: church members who defer to the wealthy and powerful. The message hits close to home and leaves no room for ambiguity.

The illustration of preferential treatment seems as relevant today as when James first wrote it, 1,900 years ago. Modern readers face the same dilemma as the first recipients of this unsettling letter. His words are easy enough to understand, but are we doing what he says?

LIFE QUESTION: *Who do you tend to show favoritism to? The rich? People of your race? Whom do you tend to look down upon?*

Converted Coward

In this you greatly rejoice, though now for a little while you may have had to suffer grief in all kinds of trials. (1 Peter 1:6)

The Gospels portray Peter cowering in the darkness the night of Jesus' trial and execution, and denying with an oath that he had ever known the man he had followed for three years. But in this letter Peter welcomes suffering as a badge of honor, proof of his commitment to Christ at any cost. Seeing the resurrected Jesus—especially in the poignant scene by a lake when Jesus reinstated him (John 21)—had changed Peter forever.

Most likely, Peter wrote this letter during an outbreak of persecution under Nero. Urgent questions stirred up within the embattled Christian community. Should they flee or resist? Should they tone down their outward signs of faith? Peter's readers, their lives in danger, needed clear advice. Beyond that, they also desired some explanation of the meaning of suffering. Why does God allow it? Does God care?

As this chapter shows, Peter's response focuses not on the *cause of suffering*—the "Why?"—but rather on the *results*. He answers that suffering can "refine" faith, much like a furnace refines impure metals. Suffering shifts attention from the rewards of this world—wealth, status, power—to more permanent, "imperishable" rewards in the life to come. And if Christians maintain their faith through persecution, a watching world will have to acknowledge the source of that faith, God himself.

Evidently, the early Christians heeded Peter's advice. More often than not, intense persecution led to a spurt of growth in the church. An ancient saying expresses this phenomenon, "The blood of martyrs is the seed of the church." According to tradition, Peter himself died a martyrs' death. He was reportedly crucified head downward on a Roman cross because he thought himself unworthy to die right side up like Jesus.

In this first chapter, Peter turns what could be a reason for despair into a reason for great hope. He sees the church, in all its birth pangs, as the long-awaited goal of the Old Testament prophets, indeed, the goal of all history.

LIFE QUESTION: *When has your faith gone through a "refining fire"?*

Hidden Dangers

As 1 Peter demonstrates, leaders of the New Testament church did not consider persecution a grave threat. To the contrary, such trials purified and strengthened the church by forcing true believers to come forward and exhibit their courage and faith.

The real dangers to the church came from within. Take the matter of unity. At the Last Supper with the disciples, Jesus had prayed that believers "may be one as we are one" (John 17:11). But within a generation, the church had splintered into followers of Paul or his rivals, legalists, free-wheelers, Judaizers, doomsdayers, and dozens of different groups.

Typically, these groups would focus on a minor doctrinal issue and waste energy on meaningless debates. This letter, for example, seems directed toward Christians obsessed with the last days. Some, impatient over unfulfilled predictions of Christ's second coming, were already beginning to scoff at the whole idea.

The author of 2 Peter has strong words of correction for such splinter groups. He reminds them that the Gospel is no fairy tale, no collection of "cleverly invented stories." As an eyewitness on the Mount of Transfiguration, he had heard God give resounding approval to his Son. If that God has promised a Second Coming, then rest assured it will take place.

As in many New Testament letters, the emphasis in 2 Peter strays back and forth between what to believe and what kind of person to be. The author lays out a progressive list of qualities— faith, goodness, knowledge, self-control, perseverance, godliness, brotherly kindness, love—that will strengthen against any temptations toward disunity.

The author of this letter is an old man, soon to face death. As a final swan song, he can do no better than remind his readers of the most basic truths of the Christian life. The answer to false knowledge is true knowledge; the answer to immoral living is moral living. As he prepares to die, the author of 2 Peter appeals one last time for truth.

LIFE QUESTION: *Of the seven qualities mentioned in 2 Peter 1:5–7, which describe your life now? Which need work?*

Sounding the Alarm

The brief letter from Jude (possibly the brother of Jesus) has much in common with 2 Peter. Both of them concern danger signs in the church, and the actual wording in Jude closely parallels that of 2 Peter 2. But Jude speaks with an even shriller tone. The disease has spread. If not arrested, it will infect the entire body.

In its approach, Jude resembles the scary movies against drugs and drunk driving that high schools sometimes show their students. They make viewers uncomfortable, which is precisely their purpose. Jude confesses that although he would prefer to write a more joyful letter about salvation, first he must alert them to the serious threat posed by certain troublemakers.

Jude doesn't elaborate on what the troublemakers were saying, but the early church was plagued by roving teachers who claimed some special "word from the Lord." Often these false teachers, seeking a profit, told audiences exactly what they wanted to hear: God's grace is so great that you can live however you want, with no penalty. Jude makes devastatingly clear what he thinks of such ideas. He calls the imposters spies and urges believers to fight for the true faith.

Ironically, only one portion of Jude gets much attention today: the beautiful doxology at the end. Evidently, Jude's strong words are no easier to take today than when they were first given.

LIFE QUESTION: *If Jude were alive today, what issues in the world might he write about in this fiery tone?*

Merest Christianity

Shortly after World War II, the brilliant Christian thinker C.S. Lewis communicated his beliefs about the faith in a series of British radio broadcasts that were then edited into the book *Mere Christianity.* He covered the basics, the bare essentials of Christian belief. Yet even that slim book would seem overly long and complex to the apostle John, author of this letter. John used the simplest language of any New Testament writer—his three letters together employed barely 300 different Greek words—to express the gospel in its most distilled form.

An early Christian writer named Jerome tells the story of John as a very old man being carried into the church at Ephesus. The people had gathered to hear a message from the famous apostle, but he would only repeat, "Little children, love one another." When asked why, he replied, "Because it is the Lord's command, and if this is done, it is enough."

That kind of single-mindedness shines through John's letters. This passage begins with wonder, astonishment even, that God has lavished his love on us. We are his children! But then John asks the obvious question: If we are God's children, why don't we act like it? Don't children of good parents naturally want to emulate them?

John was the last surviving apostle. He lived almost to the end of the first century, and may have been in his eighties when he wrote this book. Already, elite cults such as the Gnostics had sprung up within the church, and Christians were hotly debating esoteric matters of theology and ethics. John dismissed these with a wave of his hand. To him, the proof of a person's faith was perfectly obvious: "If anyone has material possessions and sees his brother in need but has no pity on him, how can the love of God be in him?" His words are as piercingly direct as the words of the Sermon on the Mount. A person who loves God acts like it; it's that simple.

LIFE QUESTION: *If you could condense the code you live by into one sentence, what would it be?*

When To Be Hospitable

KEY VERSE: *Many deceivers, who do not acknowledge Jesus Christ as coming in the flesh, have gone out into the world. Any such person is the deceiver and the antichrist. Watch out that you do not lose what you have worked for. (2 John v.7–8)*

Most early churches founded by missionaries like the apostle Paul met in private homes. Later on, Paul began sending out emissaries, like Timothy and Titus, who joined the original apostles in making "the circuit" from church to church. Christians had the practice of hosting traveling teachers in their homes, rather than making them stay in the notoriously unsafe Roman inns.

Before long, however, false teachers followed suit, bringing distortions of the original gospel and sowing confusion and discord. Soon religious racketeers joined in, seeking free food and lodging. The issue arose of what to do with the new breed of pseudo-evangelists. Should Christians offer hospitality to them, too? The letters of 2 and 3 John, the shortest letters in the New Testament, deal with this very problem.

These two letters are best read together, since each gives one side of a problem facing a young church. The book of 2 John urges Christians to use discretion in testing a visitor's message and motive. It cautions against hosting visitors who do not teach the truth about Christ. True to his nickname, the apostle of love repeats his motto, "Love one another," even in this letter of warning.

On the other hand, 3 John praises a man named Gaius for warmly welcoming genuine Christian teachers. Gaius's church was dominated by a gossipy dictator who excluded all outsiders.

In a very condensed form, John's two letters deal with heresy and church splits—two problems that have plagued the church in every age, in every place. To defend against those dangers, John stresses the need for love and discernment. Believers must know whom to accept and support, and whom to resist.

LIFE QUESTION: *Who are some modern "deceivers" or false teachers? What issues tend to provoke "church discipline" today?*

The Final Word

KEY VERSE: *"I am the Alpha and the Omega," says the Lord God, "who is, and who was, and who is to come, the Almighty." (Rev. 1:8)*

*I*magine the Bible without the book of Revelation. After the Old Testament come the four Gospels, which then lead into Acts and its account of missionary ventures, followed by the letters to the resulting churches. All fine so far, but one thing is missing: Where is history going? Where will it end up?

One would have to reach beyond all credibility to make a case that the prophets' promised kingdom of peace and righteousness has come about in the years since Jesus' Ascension. Our own century has included two World Wars, several hundred lesser wars, two atom bomb attacks, a Holocaust, and numerous mass killings by half-crazed dictators. Where is the time promised by Isaiah when swords will be beaten into plowshares and the lion will lie down by the calf?

Revelation adds a two-word message: Just wait. God is not finished with this planet. The Bible stakes God's own reputation on his ability to restore this planet to its original state of perfection. Only when that happens will history have run its course.

As the book opens, the apostle John has been banished on the island of Patmos, a hard-labor colony. In that bleak setting, he receives a vision remarkably similar in style to those reported by the prophets Ezekiel and Daniel. Many details of John's vision no one can claim to understand with confidence. But this first chapter establishes why the visions were given. John presents a new picture of Jesus.

Yes, Jesus is the babe in the manger, and the Good Shepherd, and the teacher of disciples, and the model of humanity, and the Son of God who died on a cross. But he is something else as well: He is the blazing supernatural creature whose very presence knocked John to the ground. He is the Creator of this world who will someday return to *re-create,* and make new all that humankind has spoiled.

LIFE QUESTION: *Does your "image" of Jesus include the image given in this chapter?*

Another Side of History

*I*n this passage from Revelation John uses bizarre, cosmic symbols: a pregnant woman clothed with the sun; a seven-headed red dragon so enormous that its tail sweeps a third of the stars from the sky; a flight into the desert; a war in heaven. Despite its many interpretations, almost all agree that this chapter has something to do with Jesus' birth and its effect on the universe. When a baby was born, the universe shuddered.

In a sense, Revelation 12 presents Christmas from a cosmic perspective, adding a new set of images to the familiar scenes of manger and shepherds and the Slaughter of the Innocents. What was visible on earth represented ripples on the surface; underneath, massive disruptions were shaking the foundations of the universe. Even as King Herod was trying to kill all male babies in Palestine, cosmic forces were at war behind the scenes. From God's viewpoint—and Satan's—Christmas was far more than the birth of a baby; it was an invasion, the decisive advance in the great struggle for the cosmos. Revelation depicts this struggle in terms of a murderous dragon opposing the forces of good.

Which is the "true" picture of Christmas: the account in Matthew and Luke, or that in Revelation? They are the same picture, told from two different points of view. This view of Christ's birth in Revelation 12 typifies the pattern of the entire book, in which John fuses things seen with things normally not seen. In daily life, two parallel histories occur at the same time: one on earth and one in heaven. Revelation, by parting the curtain, allows us to view them together. It leaves the unmistakable impression that, as we make everyday choices between good and evil, those choices are having an impact on the supernatural universe we cannot see.

No matter how it may appear from our limited perspective, God maintains firm control over all history. Finally, even the despots will end up fulfilling the plan mapped out for them by God.

LIFE QUESTION: *When have you ever felt part of a "spiritual warfare"?*

Return to Eden

*I*n its "plot," the Bible ends up very much where it began. The broken relationship between God and human beings has healed over at last, and the curse of Genesis 3 is lifted. Borrowing images from Eden, Revelation pictures a river and a tree of life. But this time a great city replaces the garden setting, a city filled with worshipers of God. Nothing will pollute that city; no death or sadness will ever darken that scene. There will be no crying or pain. For the first time since Eden, the *World As It Is* will finally match the *World As God Wants It*.

John saw heaven as the fulfillment of every Jewish dream: Jerusalem restored. For someone else—say a refugee in the Third World today—heaven may represent a family reunited, a home abundant with food and fresh drinking water. Heaven stands for the fulfillment of every true longing.

Revelation promises that our longings are not mere fantasies. They will come true. When we awake in the new heaven and new earth, we will have at last whatever we have longed for. Somehow, from out of all the bad news in a book like Revelation, good news emerges—spectacular Good News. A promise of goodness without a catch in it somewhere. There is a happy ending after all.

In the Bible, heaven is not an afterthought or optional belief. It is the final justification of all creation. The Bible never belittles human tragedy and disappointment—is any book more painfully honest?—but it does add the one key word *temporary*. What we feel now, we will not always feel. The time for *re-creation* will come.

For people who feel trapped in pain or in a broken home, in economic misery or in fear—for all those people, for all of us, heaven promises a future time, far longer and more substantial than the time we spend on earth, a time of health and wholeness and pleasure and peace. The Bible began with that promise in the book of Genesis. And the Bible ends with that same promise, a guarantee of future reality. The end will be a beginning.

LIFE QUESTION: *What do you long for in the re-created earth?*